The Human Skills

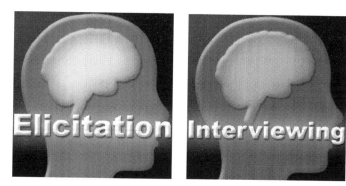
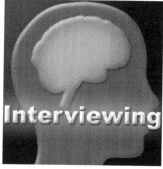

By Frank Stopa

ISBN: 9781450599856

Contents

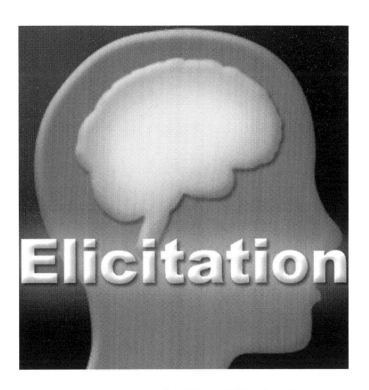

The Human Skills: Elicitation

By Frank Stopa

The Human Skills: Elicitation
Contents

Introduction

What is it that makes the difference between success and failure in almost any endeavor? Good Information is the difference. Knowing how your contacts will respond to your sales approaches could determine whether you achieve your sales goals. Good Information is at the root of that. Reading your suspect's personality and behaviors will drive the success of your interrogation and investigation. Good Information is at the root of that. Understanding how your counterparts will respond to your negotiating positions determines whether you are able to craft win-win solutions in the toughest of negotiations. Good information is at the root of that.

Whether you are working in sales or business strategy, law enforcement or intelligence, education or politics, you rely on collecting information. Good information provides the foundation for good decision-making. It stands to reason then that collecting good information, more effectively, more efficiently, and while building stronger working relationships, would help you achieve better results in everything you do. That is exactly what this book is about.

The Human Skills: Elicitation is a manual that will show you how to apply the core concepts and specific conversational techniques underlying the art and skill of maneuvering yourself through conversations to collect the information you need to make sound decisions. We will explain each technique and you will see examples of how they are applied in real world situations. We encourage you to discover each technique for yourself, to learn which ones work best for you. Then, we encourage you to experiment and practice. The more you practice, the better you will become at applying the techniques.

What is Elicitation?

Webster's New Collegiate Dictionary defines elicitation as "to draw forth or bring out, to derive by logical processes, to call forth or draw out (a response or reaction)."

For the purposes of collecting human source information, this means that elicitation can be viewed as a simple cause and effect. It begins with building a relationship, either personal or professional. Next, it continues with application of various manipulations of conversation – or "logical processes" – that draw out a response or reaction. And finally, it concludes with the passage of information from the contact to the elicitor.

This isn't all that's involved in elicitation, however. The decision to employ elicitation techniques may include a need to maintain a degree of discretion or confidentiality in your information collection efforts. Whether you intend to elicit information from a business competitor while keeping your agenda concealed; or prompt revelations from a taciturn suspect intent on concealing his involvement in a crime; or even determining your teenager's weekend plans without becoming an interrogator, the idea of concealing your information collection agenda and interests is part and parcel of elicitation. Otherwise, you could simply resort to classic – and rather blunt – question and answer techniques.

Given all of this, it is a simple matter to construct a working definition of elicitation that suits our purposes:

> *Elicitation is the collection of information from a professional or personal contact that is characterized by the development of a human relationship that sustains the employment of discreet conversational manipulation.*

How Does Elicitation Work?

Defining elicitation in written terms is one thing, but understanding how it works is the essence of this book. Elicitation is both art and science. It is a complex activity involving a basic understanding of human nature, knowledge of the techniques that render your contacts amenable to providing you with information, and practical experience in interpersonal communication.

In your efforts to collect information from others, this means first applying our Core Concepts in your interactions to build strong rapport and long-lasting relationships; then, employing our Conversational Techniques at specific moments in your conversations; and finally reaping the rewards, the information you need to make good, sound decisions.   We call this **The Elicitation Cause and Effect.**

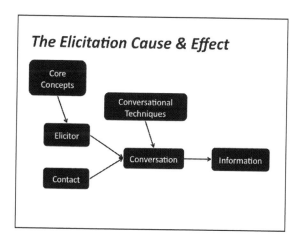

13

The Relationship

All information collection from others is rooted in the relationships you build. You may not spend months or years getting to know a professional contact, but you still build a relationship with that person. This might take place over a few weeks or a few months, or it might take place within the span of fifteen minutes. Regardless, building a relationship is the key to unlocking the information you want to collect. The stronger the relationship grows the more it facilitates the flow of information. Our battery of core concepts emphasizes the benefits of building long-lasting relationships, which sustain the exchange of all kinds of information over time. Whether you are working with one contact on a specific issue, or networking with a wide range of individuals, the informational benefits of building durable relationships is undeniable.

The core concepts encourage you to consider a range of ideas that complement your relationship building abilities, enhance your preparation, planning and risk management skills, and help you understand why people talk and why they reveal information, knowingly and unknowingly, during conversations.

The Conversational Techniques

Once you have built a relationship with a contact, and understand how and why he talks, you are ready for the 'business end' of elicitation, the employment of the "logical processes" that result in actual information collection. In practice these processes are the conversational and interrogative techniques that enable us to manipulate a conversation to collect the information we want, while preserving the relationship. These techniques include a series of discreet conversational manipulations or techniques that facilitate the flow of that information from your contact.

The Result

Finally, the result of our effort is the information. Assuring we collect what we want and need requires preparation, planning and, most importantly, attention to maintaining the relationship we have with our contact. The optimal elicitation scenario is one in which we develop a strong relationship, rely less and less every day on conversational manipulation, and seek information openly and sincerely.

Core Concepts

The Information Collection Spectrum

The Information Collection Spectrum describes a continuum of human source information collection activities, which share common techniques and concepts. They are at their foundations similar in that they all share the objective of prompting your contact to provide information. What differentiates them, one from another, are the degree of control you exercise over the interaction, including the setting, and the degree of willingness displayed by your contact in complying with your agenda, hidden or not.

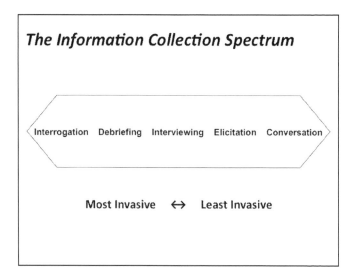

Interrogation
Interrogation is most often considered a military, intelligence or law enforcement tool to prompt a

suspect to provide intelligence information or evidence. The interrogator typically exercises control over the setting, as well as the direction, of the questioning. We often envision interrogation as a hostile activity in which the suspect displays disdain for the interrogator and an unwillingness to provide information. Although many collection techniques may be applied to interrogations, simple question and answer forms its basis.

Debriefing

Debriefing is the act of asking questions of another person to obtain useful information. Debriefing is often considered a military or intelligence tool employed in collecting battlefield or political intelligence from a soldier or a confidential informant, although similar activities take place in other fields as well. The debriefer often exercises control over the setting as well as the direction of the questioning. The soldier, informant, or other contact, is typically a willing interlocutor.

Interviewing

Interviewing covers a wide range of information collection activities, including journalistic and media interviews, job interviews, and police interviews of witnesses. The interviewer generally maintains control over the direction of the interview, although this depends to an extent on the willingness of the contact. The contact may be a job applicant willing to share any information that helps him obtain employment, or somebody resisting an overly inquisitive journalist. As for the setting, either party may influence or control where the interview takes place.

Conversation

We now jump forward on the spectrum to conversation. A conversation is an activity in which two people talk, exchange information willingly and typically do not have any initial information collection agendas. Either side may choose of suggest a setting. Both sides typically converse more or less freely, and the conversation meanders with no apparent objective.

Elicitation

The reason we jumped past Elicitation of the spectrum and looked at conversation first is that elicitation may be thought of as 'conversation with an agenda.' In addition to our previous definition of elicitation, we can characterize it as an information collection effort in which the elicitor attempts to exercise control over the direction of the conversation without revealing his agenda to his contact. As for setting, a wide range of influence may be exercised by either party as to where they converse. And finally, there may be a wide range of willingness in the contact to providing information at the elicitor's prompting.

The Planning Cycle

    The planning cycle is our simple method for assuring you maximize your information collection. First you Prepare & Plan your elicitation effort, then you Act, in other words, you collect the information you're seeking, and then you Review & Record your results.

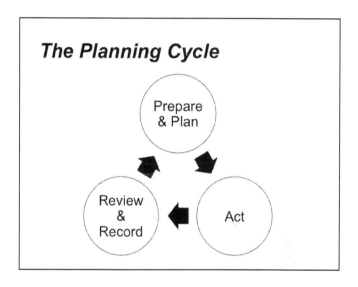

Prepare & Plan
    This phase of the Planning Cycle is all about getting yourself ready to elicit information from your contact.

Know Your Objective
    Knowing what information or what kind of information you want to collect is the first step in

determining how to go about collecting that information. This does not mean you must know exactly what information you'll obtain, but it does mean you should know what kind of result you are looking for.

Know Your Contact
People are generally more willing to engage you, if they feel at ease in your company. When you know something about your contact in advance, you have gotten over the first hurdle. The benefits of doing this should never be underestimated. This part of learning about your contact is actually the beginning of building a long-lasting relationship. As you'll see later on, we recommend you learn as much as you can about your contact's personality. The following questions will help you understand the kinds of things you might like to know.

Has your contact written anything that will help you understand his personality, beliefs, ideals, etc.?
Do you have a photograph?
What is his age? What is his age relative to you?
What are his political views?
What are his personal likes/dislikes?

| Does he prefer casual or more formal dress? |
| Is he married? Does he have children? |

Organize Your Approach

Conversations can be unpredictable, usually taking you in unexpected directions. Preparing an agenda will assist you in making sense of those unexpected directions, quickly allowing you to determine what information you have collected and what opportunity or potential remains in the conversation. We recommend you prepare notes and questions. Even if you can't use them during your conversation, writing them down will permit you to assimilate them, to have that information at your disposal when it counts most.

Practice

To the extent possible, we recommend you review your notes, rehearse your questions, and anticipate your contact's reactions. There is a saying in war, that "no plan survives contact with the enemy." The same is true of any activity based on human interaction; your conversations will never play out as you had envisioned. If you've made an honest attempt to anticipate the unexpected, you will be better prepared to handle it when things don't play out as planned.

Act

This is the conversation during which you carry out your elicitation. It is during this phase of the Planning Cycle that you will reconfirm what you know, or don't know, about your contact; apply the Core Concepts we will examine in the next chapter to understand how to maneuver through the conversation; and employ the conversational techniques that will allow you to collect the information you want.

Review & Record

We believe strongly that you should review your results immediately, document them in some way, and then plan for next opportunity. Your elicitation efforts will include encounters for which you are able to plan your actions to maximize the collection of information, and they will include impromptu meetings during which you meet a contact for the first time. This will result in a wide range of experiences as well as results. Reviewing those experiences and results, and documenting them, will develop in you a sense of strategy to your efforts. You will begin collecting bits and pieces of information from various contacts, which together form a comprehensive picture. You will also being to learn valuable lessons about your own elicitation skills, which will help you improve. The following questions may help you review your encounters.

What did you learn about your contact?
How does it compare with what I already know?
What will you attempt to learn about him the next time?

What did you NOT learn or collect?
What will you attempt to learn the next time?

Recording your results is every bit as important as reviewing them. With the amounts of information we deal with every day and way we network constantly, meeting new people both face to face and virtually, it is becoming more and more difficult to keep everything organized in our minds. Therefore, documenting your results in some way is almost an imperative. Now, this doesn't mean you have to create a 'dossier' on everyone you meet. What it does mean is you should take advantage of some of the various address book and contacts applications that all of our smart phones and laptops make available to us.

Finally, it is worth mentioning that the benefit of reviewing and recording your results is that you can quickly compare those results against your collection agenda. This allows you to more easily plan what and how to obtain the remaining information. Planning for the next collection opportunity brings you full circle in the Planning Cycle.

The Structured Interview

The Structured Interview is less an actual structure for conducting an interview or than it is a general guide to the flow most human interaction follows. While no two human interactions are ever the same, most do share some basic characteristics. These include the greeting, the actual interaction and the closing. Since we are specifically looking at interactions during which you are attempting to collect information, we have chosen to extend the interaction portion into three steps, which we will call Listening, Asking and the Recap.

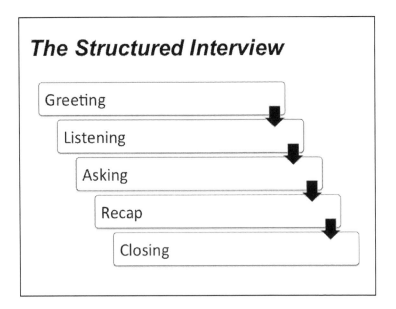

Greeting

The Greeting is the opening phase of the conversation. As you might surmise, it's all about putting your contact at ease and setting the stage to collect information. The greeting begins quite literally with the greeting, welcoming you contact, exchanging pleasantries and building rapport. The goal is to put your contact at ease, because when people feel comfortable, they are much more amenable to sharing information.

The greeting concludes with setting the stage for your information collection agenda. This entails explaining your interests. In a friendly conversation, this might be nothing more than expressing your desire to enjoy your contact's company. In a police interrogation it might entail explaining much more blatantly your objective of determining the suspect's guilt or innocence. The key here is to gently channel your contact into the frame of mind in which he is predisposed to provide you information.

Finally, please keep in mind that the Greeting can be a short exchange of "hello's", it can be a curt business-like handshake, or it can be an hour-long procession through rapport building and re-establishing relationships that is common in other parts of the world. Whichever end of the spectrum you come from, you can't avoid the Greeting. Make the most of it.

Listening

The next phase of the conversation is what we call Listening. This is when you allow your contact to have the attention. Nobody likes being 'talked at'. People prefer to be able to express themselves.

While you may be trying to collect specific kinds of information, there will often be times when your contact will open your eyes to new information, or a new perspective on your subject. Let that happen, you can always return later to your agenda items.

The bottom line is you'll never know what you don't know, unless you ask. Another benefit this has for your interview is the way seeking input from your contact helps achieve a degree of "buy in" to your agenda. In other words, if he feels like you are making him feel important enough to be consulted during the interview, he will likely work harder in identifying the information that matters most to you.

Asking

This now brings you to the pursuit of your information collection agenda. Once you've set the stage for your interview or debriefing, this is when you actually collect the information you need. Here, you manage the conversation to take on topics of interest to you that help satisfy your collection agenda. As you are able to develop more fluidity in your conversation, you may then employ the conversational techniques, which more finely tune your collection effort.

Recap

Your penultimate step emphasizes the need to review the work you have done with your contact. This is intended to assure that you have collected the information correctly. One truth about collecting information your contact is that its transmission is often subject to your perceptions of what your contact provided. If you've ever played a word game in which people pass on a story from one person to the next until the last person is asked to repeat the story and discover how it has changed, then you know how even the simplest information can be distorted through passage from one person to another. Reviewing what you have collected with your contact ensures that you have correctly perceived it. It is in this stage that you can correct mistakes in specific pieces of information, ensure your understanding of the facts, and account for differences in perception of that information between you and your contact.

Closing

Finally, we come to the close of the meeting. This is when you thank your contact for taking the time to meet with you. But this is not all that you do. You also continue to develop rapport and lay the groundwork for future meetings. Anybody who works with people on a regular basis knows the importance of building a relationship. You just never know when you'll need to ask a contact, friend or acquaintance for a favor, or for information. You'll never know when the friendly relationship you built will pay off in terms of a sale. You'll never know when you will need to or want to call on your contact for more information. Do yourself a favor. Don't alienate your interlocutor, always leave the possibility for future contact open - it may pay dividends some day.

Human Motivations

In the 1950's, American Psychologist Abraham Maslow described the broad categories of needs we as human beings seek to satisfy as we mature and develop. He constructed his description as a hierarchy and, thus, named it the Hierarchy of Needs. For you, the Hierarchy of Needs is a road map to your contact's motivations, which can help you determine how to craft your elicitation efforts.

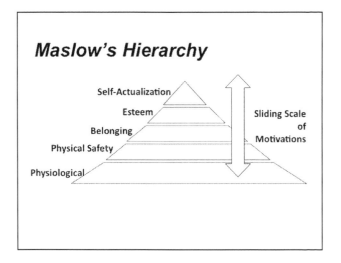

The Hierarchy of needs begins with the satisfaction of the survival needs, and progresses upward through our various physical and spiritual needs. These include the search for love, status, self-esteem and, finally, self-actualization. They are important in terms of elicitation, as they provide a road map to the desires and tendencies you may be able to work with to motivate your contact to respond with the information you want. These needs, desires and tendencies include:

Physiological

These are the basic physiological needs, the food air and water we need to survive as biological entities. They are our survival needs. Most people have developed the ability to satisfy these basic needs through their participation in society. They have employment, which puts food on the table, pays the rent, and allows them to have normal social lives.

When the ability to assure survival is put at risk, strong motivations come into play. These will often change dramatically your contact's willingness to discuss previously sensitive or personal topics, allowing for the elicitation of information. You might have seen this in a person that has lost his job, or a suspect who has lost his freedom after arrest, or even someone who is hungry. If you have, you know someone amenable to elicitation.

Characteristics You Might See
Hunger, Thirst
Need for Work, a Job
Desire for Freedom from Incarceration

Physical Safety

The physical safety needs are an extension of the physiological needs. They encompass a range of needs including clothing and shelter, protection from physical and emotional harm, as well as living in a society that enforces the rule of law and respect for individual rights. Once a person is able to satisfy his most basic physiological, or survival, needs, he will seek to satisfy the physical needs. Having clothing, shelter and a predictable existence provided by a society build on laws enables to more easily satisfy his physiological needs on a daily basis.

Consider the person who scrapes by in a war zone whose basic ability to provide for his family has been compromised, or the flood victim, dealing daily with looters and vandals. How about the maturing criminal seeking a way out of his illegal existence, or the community member having to cope with gang and drug activity in his own neighborhood? These people are faced with challenges to their ability to maintain a predictable, settled life and will likely be amenable to elicitation.

Characteristics You Might See
Desire for a Safe Place to Live
Desire for Freedom from Incarceration
Freedom from Pursuit (by the police)
Predictable Daily Life
Desire for a Safe Community
Regular Employment
Need to 'Right a Wrong'
Desire for 'Justice' to be done

Belonging

At this stage on the hierarchy, we seek affection, love, belonging, acceptance and friendship from others. We are social beings and thrive when our affiliations with others allows us to maximize our potential in satisfying the physiological and physical safety needs. To do this, people live in families, and belong to professional, social, religious and political groups and organizations. They want to feel as if they are participating and contributing members of those groups.

When a person lacks those affiliations, he seeks them out. We've all met people who are looking or a friend, who aren't taken seriously in their jobs, who are underappreciated or misunderstood. Can you easily chat with someone like this? You can; he is definitely amenable to elicitation.

Characteristics You Might See
Desire to fit in
Need for a Friend, Someone to Talk to
Need for Affection, Love
Desire to Make a Contribution to Society/Group
Desire for Something to Believe in
Need to Please People
Naïveté

Esteem

Once a person is able to fulfill his needs for food, water, shelter and clothing in a predictable way and through his affiliations with family, friends and co-workers, he then seeks their respect, recognition and attention. He seeks to gratify his ego. He seeks power, fame, and money. This is the esteem phase of the hierarchy. As in the previous phases, the pursuit of satisfying these needs also creates strong influences, which render him vulnerable to your elicitation efforts.

Have you ever met a person who craves the attention of others, or maybe someone who wants everyone to know how well informed or influential he is, or someone who simply has a big ego and wants everyone to know it? If this reminds you of your contact, then you know someone amenable to elicitation.

Characteristics You Might See
Strong Ego
Need to be perceived as a Professional
Need for Attention
Ambition (too much)
Need for Personal Recognition
Tendency to Gossip or Brag
Need for Affection
Desire for Power, Leadership
Desire for Monetary Reward
Desire to Seek Revenge

Self-Actualization

This is the pinnacle of Maslow's Hierarchy of Needs. This is the stage at which an individual has fulfilled the all of the preceding needs and seeks to satisfy the need to develop his identity, his raison d'être. In his 1954 book Motivation and Personality, Maslow states, "What a man can be, he must be." It

34

is at this stage that an individual understands his abilities, his place in society, as well as the contributions he may make. He is self-actualized.

At this stage, there appears to be little of value in terms of identifying characteristics or needs that can be exploited for elicitation. However, there is one characteristic of Maslow's Hierarchy of Needs that you must keep in mind before deciding your contact is invulnerable to your elicitation efforts – the Sliding Scale of Motivations.

Characteristics You Might See
Desire or Need to Teach, Educate

The Sliding Scale of Motivations

In his research, Maslow recognized that elite performers, those who self-actualize, tend to feel self-actualized at some moments and not at others in accordance with the needs they seek to satisfy at any given time. In other words, the hierarchy of needs is a dynamic, ever-changing hierarchy in which individuals may seek self-actualization in one moment and then have physiological needs in the next. We called this ever-changing state, the Sliding Scale of Motivations.

A martial arts master may be self-actualized in terms of his art, but still needs to satisfy the more basic needs; he gets tired and needs to eat, drink and rest. He needs to attract paying customers to his dojo or risk closing his business. Osama Bin Laden, the notorious terrorist leader, may be the quintessential self-actualized jihadist much of the time, but he's still on the run and needs to look after his personal safety all of the time. The lesson for you is that your contact has a wide variety of needs that must be attended to throughout his life. The challenge is to identify those needs and then play on them in your elicitation efforts.

Memory: First & Last

There is an important concept we'd like you to remember.

People tend to remember the first & last things they hear.

The field of Cognitive Psychology is a discipline with the broader field of Psychology, which examines the internal mental processes of thought including visual processing, language, problem solving, and memory. We are specifically interested in cognitive psychological theories as they pertain to memory in order to achieve two possible outcomes – to enhance the probability that your contact will remember what he discussed with you, or to decrease the probability that your contact will remember what he discussed with you. Remembering a conversation with you, or portions of it, may be important for your contact when you are forging a relationship. Forgetting a conversation, or more specifically forgetting potions of it, may be important for you in terms of protecting your agenda and interests; you may recall that the elicitation of information is intended to be a discreet

36

manipulation of conversation. The focus here is on discreet.

Trace Decay Theory

Trace decay theory, as posited by Peterson and Peterson in 1959, suggests that our short-term memory is only capable of containing a small amount of information in the form of memories for a short period of time – somewhere on the order of tens of seconds. Unless we process, or encode, those short-term memories into our long-term memory, they will decay until they are lost.

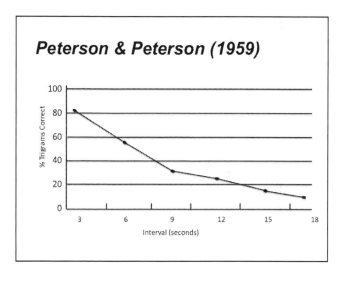

Interference Theory

Interference theory as posited by Dr. B.J. Underwood in 1957 explains that we tend to forget information in short-term memory when they are subjected to interference from previously learned information or newly learned information. Experiments conducted by Underwood and

Peterson and Peterson suggest that in the former case, information you have learned before encoding new, similar information into long-term memory can worsen recall of the new information. This is called proactive interference. Similarly, when newly learned information conflicts or interferes with more recently learned information, the more recent information tends to obscure or overwrite the previous information. This is called retroactive interference.

Displacement Theory

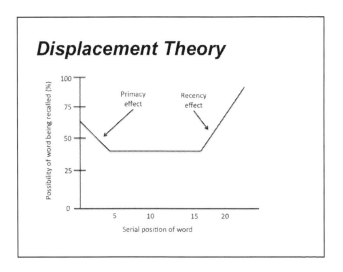

Displacement theory postulates that people tend to retain information in short-term memory longer, hence making it available for encoding into long-term memory, when encountered at the beginning or the end of some event, a list, a statement or an activity, etc. Information at the beginning of the event tends to be held in short-term memory long <u>enough</u> to be rehearsed and thus encoded and retained in long-term memory, while information at the end of the event is not subject to interference from new information and is thus easier to retain for encoding.

Information in the middle of the event tends to be obscured, or more easily forgotten, by proactive or retroactive interference, meaning those pieces of information preceding or succeeding it.

Encoding Information

The act of processing new information from our short-term memory into our long-term memory is called encoding. It is this encoding that allows us to store memories, knowledge, information, etc. According her 2000 book, <u>Brain Matters: Translating Research into Classroom Practice</u>, educational consultant Dr. Patricia Wolfe estimates that most human beings sift through the information they receive retaining something on the order of only 1% for encoding into long-term memory. The information we encode tends to be that which receives our attention. In other words, if we are prompted to think about or discuss the information, we will tend to remember it. If we repeat the information, we tend to remember it. If we collect the information through multiple sensory inputs, i.e. seeing it and hearing it, we tend to remember it. And, if we can associate or link that information with previous memories, we tend to remember it.

Do you want him to remember?

So, what this all means for us is that if you want to increase the probability that your contact will remember the substance of your conversation, there are several things you can do. First, provide the information you want him remember in small chunks and allow time for him to encode it. Second, repeat or revisit the information. This allows him to associate the information with previous memories. Third, to the extent possible, present the information in multiple sensory formats. And finally, present the information at the beginning and/or the conclusion of the conversation to enhance retention in short-term memory.

Do you want him to forget?
Conversely, if you are interested in protecting your agenda and focusing your contact's attention away from what you just discussed, you do much the opposite. First, place your important discussion in the middle of the conversation. Second, present the information in only one format to reduce the chances encoding will take place. Third, do not revisit the topic. Allow it to 'fade' from memory. And finally, present information in lengthier pieces with little to no time between pieces for encoding into long-term memory.

Observation

Before you ever meet your contact, you need to prepare and plan as much as you can. The first step in successfully eliciting information effort is to know your contact. This eases building rapport and a successful relationship. It also helps you select the right mix of elicitation techniques. Some of the things you would like to learn may be readily available in open source information. Some might need to be discerned through observation, before or during the elicitation.

Questions you might like to answer before you meet your contact
Gender?
What is his job or position?
How old is he?
What is his educational background?
Was he in the military, the police, or government service in a prior career?
Has he traveled?
Do you have a photograph?
What are his economic, political, religious or viewpoints?

Has he published anything?
What are his likes and dislikes?
Does he have any hobbies or pastimes?
Does he have any habits, such as drinking or smoking?
Does he prefer casual or more formal attire?
Is he married, with a family?
Is he introverted or extroverted?
Is he egotistic and self-centered, or is he unselfish and humble?

While in today's world, you may be able to answer some of these questions through online research, or by talking with acquaintances of your contact, you will have to answer many of them through your own direct observation of and conversation. This is an important part of assessing him and deciding which elicitation techniques work best at which times.

Questions you should try to answer for yourself during direct observation and conversation

Is he a fastidious dresser, or is he unconcerned with the details?
Does he look at the world strategically from the top down, or is he more tactical, from the bottom up?
Does he talk in terms of himself, or does he refer to others?
Does he process information through visual, auditory, or sensory inputs?
How does he interact with subordinates, superiors, and colleagues?
How concerned is he about what others think of him and his actions?
What motivates him to succeed?
Is his nature warm, open and welcoming, or is he suspicious, cold and defensive?
Does he display photos of his family in his office?
Does he display awards or other recognition in his office?

> Does he drive an expensive or moderate vehicle?

The answers to all of these questions, collected over time, before, during and after your meetings will help you develop a clear assessment of your contact, what motivates him, and how he might be amenable to your efforts to elicit information from him.

Active Listening

It is said that 60% of problems that between people and within businesses are communications problems. Madelyn Burley-Allen, in her book Listening, The Forgotten Skill, asserts that 40% of the time spent in interpersonal communication is spent listening. This means that 24% of all interpersonal communications problems can be thought of as being problems in listening.

That's almost 25%! That means that where your inability to close deals, make sales, reach mutually beneficial negotiating outcomes, overcome internal personnel management problems, transfer and share human knowledge, collect information and develop a competitive advantage, and more, could be improved by almost 25%!

Can you imagine the added value you would bring to your business if you could reduce that percentage to say 15%? How about 10%? What's that worth to your bottom line? As you can see, listening effectively is critical to improving your performance.

The amazing thing about listening is that it is not difficult to improve your ability. All you need to do is follow a few simple guidelines and develop good listening habits. Over time you will notice that you learn more about and from your contacts.

What is involved in Listening?

Let's look at three basic components of active listening. These are Comprehension, Evaluation, and Response.

Comprehension is the act of understanding the message that the speaker wishes to impart. The understanding of a given piece of information depends upon the perceptions you bring to the conversation. To the extent they are the same as the speaker's perceptions, you will correctly comprehend the meaning. To the extent you have developed knowledge of your contact, as well as built a relationship with him, you will understand better and better those basic perceptions that impact the meaning of a particular piece of information.

Another aspect of comprehension is listening to non-verbal signals. Non-verbal signals can be as important as verbal responses. If you've ever noticed the physical reactions people have when you converse with them, you know what we are talking about. When people listen to you and absorb what you have to say, they are usually more relaxed. They show greater interest. They are often more personable and open to your suggestions. They face you directly. They make more frequent eye contact. On the other hand, those who do not listen do not make eye contact. They 'close' their bodies. They might cross their arms and legs. They may not face you directly. They may be tense and resistant to cooperation and collaboration. They are less personable, and do not seem to have an interest in what you're saying.

Evaluation is the next activity in active listening. Evaluation is the process of determining whether or not the message the speaker imparted fulfills your objectives. In other words, are you collecting the information you wanted to collect? Is the information relevant to the interview or debriefing? Does it add anything new to what you already know? If it does not respond to your question, or doesn't add anything new, what exactly is the response? What information is was imparted? Answering these questions for yourself as you proceed through a conversation is important in determining whether or not you are meeting your information collection objectives.

Finally, we move on to Response. Response is the act of demonstrating that you are actively engaged in the communication. It involves showing interest in the information, as well as interest in the effort made by the speaker to provide you that information. This not only requires your silence to display that you are listening. It also requires verbal and non-verbal responses to the speaker to prove that you are engaged. If you omit these responses, your contact will soon perceive that you are disinterested and lose interest himself. Once he's lost interest, you don't get any more information!

Questions to Keep in Mind as You Listen

If you keep the following questions in mind during your conversations, you will assure you comprehend and are properly evaluating what you hear.

Questions to Keep in Mind as You Listen
Is it clear to me what the response means?
What exactly is my contact saying?
Is the information relevant to my question?
Is the response complete?
Does the tone of voice carry any meaning or significance?
How does my contact feel about the response?
Is the response really the truth?
Should I interrupt now or wait until later?

Other Effective Listening Techniques

Don't Interrupt

Have you ever been on the verge of getting a thought out in a conversation when somebody cuts you off? Did you feel like he curtailed your thought, because he probably didn't care about what you were saying? Of course you did. More than likely, he wasn't really listening to you as much as he was thinking about what he wanted to say.

When you're on the listening end of a conversation allow your contact to get through what he wants to say. You might be surprised by the information you obtain. Allowing him to complete his thoughts also gives you the time to formulate better questions. You also send the non-verbal message that you are genuinely interested in what he has to say.

Clarifiers

Clarifying questions, comments or prompts are valuable in two ways. First, they help you assure you understand what your contact is saying. And second, they serve as positive responses to your contact, i.e. that you are listening and are interested. Repeat your contact's key words (see the restatement technique) or rephrase them in your own words to assure he was heard and understood. Clarifiers may also be used to prompt your contact for more detail.

Clarifiers
"Let me see if I understand…"
"If I understand correctly, what you're saying is…"

"I'm intrigued. Tell me more about..."
"I'm confused, does that mean..."
"That's interesting. Would you explain the background to that?"
"Right. And what would the implications of that be for...?"

Put Your Ego to the Side

Most people like those who listen to them. Understanding this is another important lesson you can learn about improving your listening skills. This is because most people want to be the center of attention and actively pursue that attention. This stems from a basic desire to be liked, appreciated, and understood. Think about instances when somebody interrupted you. More than likely they were succumbing to the natural urge to seek attention. Most people don't even realize they're doing it. In fact, we all do it from time to time.

If your goal were to elicit information from your contact, it would be counterproductive to compete with each other for the other's attention. When you compete for attention communication falters and information ceases to flow. The next time you are conversing with a friend, try NOT to seek his attention. Allow him to win yours. You'll be rewarded for your efforts.

Counter Elicitation

Counter Elicitation is a simple concept. It is the defense against hostile elicitation tactics. The concept recognizes that for every time you attempt to conceal your agenda or to collect information from a contact unwittingly using elicitation techniques, somebody else may be doing the same thing to you: what you can do to them, they can do to you. It also recognizes that, if you have proprietary, classified, sensitive or personal information that you wish to protect, you can do so employing a few common sense techniques.

(Note: Please recognize, however, that not all elicitation is hostile. In fact, most is completely harmless, intended only to prompt somebody to open up during conversation. It is not intended to steal your competitive secrets.)

Protection

The first step in developing techniques to defend against hostile elicitation is to recognize why you are a target of hostile elicitation. Consider the following questions, the answer to which might help you assess your status as a target.

Protection
What critical information do you need to protect?
Why do you need to protect it?

Who do you need to protect it from?
If asked specifically about a protected or personal piece of information, how would you respond?
How would you deflect that request?

Defensive Techniques

The next step in countering hostile elicitation efforts is to recognize that you have the power to deflect those efforts through the use of a few simple techniques.

- **Limited Responses**
- **Feigning Ignorance**
- **Practiced Responses**
- **Rerouting the Conversation**

Limited Responses

Limited responses to your contact's questions and efforts to elicit information are intended to make it painfully slow for him to draw you out on a particular topic. With this technique, you provide short responses containing as little information as is practical under the circumstances. This provides your contact little upon which to build viable follow on conversation, and forces him to ask more and more questions to satisfy his collection agenda.

If you return to what we mentioned about avoiding questions, you will recall that,

'During conversations, people are turned off by too many questions. They become defensive. The more questions you ask, the more you reach your contact's saturation point – the point at which you are perceived to be interrogating your contact.'

Any good elicitor will know that he can't ask an unlimited number of questions. Otherwise, he himself will perceive that he's interrogating you, and will back off.

Feigning Ignorance
Feigning Ignorance is our equivalent of the "Negotiator's Trick." This is the technique used by the savvy negotiator when confronted with aggressive, domineering negotiating counterparts. He regains the initiative by slowing him down, by asking questions, and feigning ignorance. This has the tendency to break the aggressive counterpart's rhythm, and to deflect him from his "scheduled" agenda. It tends to ruin the aggressive counterpart's day.

You can do the same thing to hostile elicitors. We've already talked about preparing & planning your elicitation, knowing your contact, and using a variety of conversational techniques. Successful elicitors do all of this and will use it on you! Every time you can derail an elicitor's pursuit of his agenda, you derail his planning & preparation, and you ruin his timing. This allows you to take control of the conversation.

Practiced Responses

> *"The grey-haired man was obviously the woman's inferior... It was nothing like so urbane nor nearly as copious as her conversation, a steady, lively flow, not of anything so coarse as direct enquiry but of remarks that would have elicited information if Stephen had chosen to give it. He did not choose, of course: after so long a course of discretion his mind would scarcely agree to give the exact time without an effort. <u>But obvious unwillingness to speak was quite as indiscreet as blabbing.</u>"*
>
> *-Patrick O'Brian,*
> *<u>The Nutmeg of Consolation</u>*

The end of this quote from Patrick O'Brian's famous Master and Commander series of novels is instructive for your counter elicitation purposes. When you are the target of a hostile elicitor, what you do NOT say is just as important as what do say.

The key to the practiced response technique is to know what you can say and cannot say, anticipate what hostile elicitors might try to collect from you, and prepare and practice responses that divert them.

Rerouting the Conversation

Rerouting the conversation is the technique of taking charge of the conversation and thwarting your contact's elicitation by changing the topic, plain and simple. Just because your contact wants to talk about a particular subject doesn't mean you have to oblige him. Practice using a variety of segues leading into new conversational topics.

> "That's really quite fascinating, but it doesn't really touch on my interests…"

> "That's clearly something that intrigues you. I, however, am a simple person. I prefer to discuss…"

Alternatively, you might also simply employ excuses to cut off the conversation before your contact puts you into an uncomfortable position. Be creative, anything will do, such as:

- **Feigning illness, a headache**
- **Feigning disinterest**
- **Leaving for an appointment**
- **A Family commitment, etc.**

An important point to note here is that in rerouting a conversation you have the choice to act, to take control, and you can. You also have the choice to act brazenly or politely. In the former case, you might not be concerned about maintaining any semblance of rapport with your contact. In the latter, maintaining the relationship may be important to you. You can do either. The power is in your hands.

The Conversational Techniques

Avoid Questions

> *"The grey-haired man was obviously the woman's inferior... (His inquiry) was nothing like so urbane nor nearly as copious as her conversation, a steady, lively flow, not of anything so coarse as direct enquiry but of remarks that would have elicited information..."*
>
> *-Patrick O'Brian, The Nutmeg of Consolation*

During conversations, people are turned off by too many questions. They become defensive. The more questions you ask, the more you reach your contact's saturation point – the point at which you are perceived to be interrogating your contact. You're no longer a conversationalist. Your contact stops responding and may begin to suspect your motives for asking so many questions.

The solution is to rephrase your questions as comments and then provide plenty of silence for him to respond. Your contact will tend to provide a response even though you have not asked a question, and will not feel like he's been interrogated. The key to this technique is all in the timing. First, you must allow your comment to hang there. And second, you must resist the temptation to add more commentary; allow your contact to respond.

An additional consideration in avoiding questions is that your contact will tend to remember the questions you asked in the conversation. To the extent you wish to reduce the focus on your interests, you can achieve this by reducing the number of questions you ask.

Examples

The following examples compare and contrast the use of too many questions and the avoidance of questions in talking with your contact.

In this example, you can see how the use of a question starts George thinking about why Robert was talking about Alpha's problems. Once Robert worked his way to the root of the elicitation and found a new and interesting angle, he immediately asked a question that betrayed more than a passing interest in the SEC's alleged investigation of Alpha. That raised suspicions in George who decided it was time to end the discussion.

Robert: I've heard that Alpha Company's stock has really faltered not because of its drop in earnings this quarter, but because of an impending SEC investigation into its accounting practices.

George: Oh really! That's interesting, because I have a neighbor who works in Alpha's headquarters office. He mentioned the same thing to me the other day.

Robert: Interesting! Did he comment at all about why the SEC decided to investigate them?

George: I don't recall all that he said. I guess we'll just have to wait and see how it comes out.

Now look at the following example and note how it differs from the previous one. There are no questions involved. You'll note that Robert doesn't ask a single question, but manages to collect much more information than in the first example. He avoids asking questions and uses comments to lead George into providing more and more insights into Alpha's problems. This is because most people will respond to your comments, if you allow them. Let your comments tail off, and follow them with plenty of silence. Most people are too polite to allow the conversation to just hang there.

Robert: I've heard that Alpha Company's stock has really faltered not because of its drop in earnings this quarter, but because of an impending SEC investigation into its accounting practices.

George: Oh really! That's interesting, because I have a neighbor who works in Alpha's headquarters office. He mentioned the same thing to me the other day.

Robert: Well, I suppose they're going to have a tough time of it for a while.

George: You're not kidding. He told me that the investigation is going to find some wrongdoing that goes right to the top of the company.

Robert: Boy, I guess when you make a mistake it's one thing, but when everybody makes mistakes...

The following phrases may be used to start your comments or to rephrase your questions.

- I would imagine that...
- It would seem to me that...
- I suppose...
- It seems like common sense that...
- Common sense would dictate...
- He couldn't possibly think that...

Provocative Statements

> *"Great questions are like that. They're provocative, forcing you to look beyond the obvious, to analyze, assess and make decisions."*
>
> *-Jill Konrath, 'Are You Asking Provocative Questions"*
> *www.evancarmichael.com*

In using the provocative statement technique you purposely make a statement that will provoke a response or reaction from your contact. In practice, you will typically drive your contact into either agreeing or disagreeing with you, putting him "on the fence." You treat the statement as a sort of multiple-choice question, which has only two possible responses, either in line with what you are saying, or the opposite of what you are saying.

In responding, your contact will typically reveal some piece of information to you, or display his feelings or opinions. Often, you may follow this with other techniques intended to draw further explanation out of him.

The provocative statement technique is a particularly valuable tool to assess your contact's political, religious or business views, as well as to assess his personality, including extroversion or introversion and NLP preferences.

Examples

If you suspected your two biggest competitors were involved in merger negotiations and wanted to seek some confirmation of that, you might consider making a provocative statement to someone you knew in one or the other firm, whom you might suspect would react in a noticeable way.

In the following example, Mark elicits the response that he wants, an indication that Betafirm and Gamma are negotiating a take over. Using the provocative statement in this way is risky in the sense that, if Mark and Walter had not built a strong relationship over time, Mark's provocation might have the long-term effect of degrading the relationship.

Mark: ...I know what you mean. Betafirm is in pretty bad shape right now. They're ripe for a takeover. In fact, I would be surprised if you

guys at Gamma weren't working on that as we speak!

Walter: (Walter turns blushes, not knowing how to respond, and remains silent for an extra moment or two.)

Mark: It's true, isn't it?

Walter: Yeah, we are looking at a takeover.

In this second example, John is first attempting to gather insights into David's NLP preferences for visual, auditory or sensory cues. Next, he'll make a statement designed to prompt David for insights into his opinion of Gamma Corporation's decision to merge with Betafirm. (David works for Gamma.)

John: What I've seen in the press suggests that the negotiations between Gamma and Betafirm have been heated and contentious. I'm sure you view it that way as well. They can't really be seeing things eye to eye.

David: They're not. The tone of the discussions is loud, with constant pounding on the table, and arguing. You can't even hear yourself think sometimes. It's not a lot of fun.

John: I get the feeling your CEO's decision to enter the talks wasn't the best. I've got to wonder about his abilities.

David: Oh I wouldn't say that. He's been great for the company. He's just having difficulty with Betafirm. We all love him and the way he's running our company.

In this example, Anna chooses to employ a provocative statement combined with disbelief based on publicly available information.

Anna: "You know Jim, I find it fascinating that you guys claim to have developed such a definitive HIV drug. So many researchers have been working on this for so long without success that it just seems strange to me you could have come up with the solution so quickly."

Jim: "I can understand how you feel about our rapid success, but I assure you we've done our homework. In fact, prior to the laboratory research, we spent three years researching what had already been done outside our firm. We've always felt on solid ground and our in house research has now borne that out."

Anna: "Come on! What about clinical trials? You haven't even launched them yet, but you're so confident you've found the cure!"

Jim: "Well that part is true. We're confident the trials will be successful. But honestly it's all based on lab research thus far."

False Statements

You can use false statements to draw information out of your contact by playing on his tendency to correct your inaccuracy. Essentially, you set the stage for a discussion of the topic in question. At the appropriate time, you make the false statement ostensibly as part of the discussion. In reality, however, you will have made the statement knowing that your interlocutor will want to make sure that the details are correct. Your goal is to prompt him or her to respond by correcting you with the accurate information.

This technique is particularly useful in eliciting information from technically oriented individuals like scientists, researchers, and engineers. They will more often than not correct you, because of a desire to see that you "got it right" or that you understood their work

Examples

In this example, Harry is attempting to elicit from Tom a confirmation that Tom's firm is able to produce aircraft landing gear at $200,000 per plane. They have already been engaged in a discussion on the topic.

Harry: "Well I presume that you guys are able to make a healthy profit on your landing gear or you wouldn't be in the business."

Mark: "Of course we do."

Harry: "Then, given all the other costs, you must be producing them at a cost of around... I suppose $150,000 per plane. Boy what profits you must be making!"

Mark: "Well, it's not really that good. Actually, the figure is more like $200,000. Our suppliers have really been increasing their prices, especially on raw materials, like titanium metal. We keep the prices down as much as we can, but there's only so much we can do."

In this example, Detective Gregory is a police detective interrogating Johnson, a suspect in a credit card fraud scheme. He knows Johnson has been left as the scapegoat, as the rest of the perpetrators have fled the country. In an attempt to prompt Johnson to provide details on the scope of the scheme, he uses a false statement.

Gregory: I was quite surprised to see that your compatriots fled the country leaving you as the fall guy.

Johnson: You were surprised! How about me? I'm the one who's going to do time!

Gregory: And for what? I estimate you couldn't have made more than $100,000 on the whole plan. It seems like peanut to me.

Johnson: $100,000! What are you kidding me? That's just what we brought in last month, man!

Gregory: That can't be. We've got receipts totaling about $99,000.

Johnson: Yeah well you're not considering all the purchases for stuff under $25. That adds up really fast! Then there are the online purchases we made at foreign retailers. As I said, we've been doing $100,000 a month for at least the last year, man!

Naïveté

Naïveté is a technique that you employ in elicitation scenarios portraying yourself as poorly informed in an effort to prompt your contact to provide insight into the topic of discussion. Care must be exercised so as not to portray your self as completely lacking knowledge or being just a bit too knowledgeable.

In the former instance, you run the risk of signaling to your contact that you aren't capable of following the conversation. Should this be the case, he may change the subject in an effort to identify a topic of conversation more suitable to you – and not related to your objectives. Or worse, he may decide that you are in fact a total idiot and abandon the conversation, leaving you with no useful information.

In the latter case, you inadvertently signal to your interlocutor in some way that you know more than you are letting on. This could lead him to conclude that you have an ulterior motive and possibly an information collection agenda. This may close off your opportunity.

Your best course of action is to know enough about the broader topic to be able to ask for more information, but not to be knowledgeable enough to portray yourself as involved in the specifics.

One caveat that we wish to make about using the naïveté technique concerns vocabulary. In many circumstances, using appropriate vocabulary assists in developing rapport and proving your interest and/or involvement. It actually helps you pursue your information collection objectives. However, in using the naïveté technique, you are pretending that you do not understand the topic. Be careful not to use specific vocabulary in the conversation. Nothing will betray your ulterior interests more than inadvertently revealing that you know more than you say. Our best advice is to allow your contact to provide you the vocabulary you need.

Example

The following example from a cocktail party may prove helpful in showing you how to tow this middle line. Mark is interested in eliciting information from Jim on security systems. He's interested in installing one at low cost, but doesn't want to appear ignorant in his first business contact the following week. The difficulty is that Jim works for the firm Mark will be negotiating with next week. He does not want to reveal his interests to Jim at this time.

Mark: Hello. So how are you enjoying this evening?

Jim: Fine, fine. And you?

Mark: Great. Our host always puts his best foot forward in these kinds of affairs.

Jim: He sure does. I'm Jim by the way. Jim Oleander.

Mark: Nice to meet you Jim. I'm Mark Downey. What do you do Jim?

Jim: I'm in security work. I'm a risk analysis expert for Alpha Company's Security Division.

Mark: That sounds like an interesting field.

Jim: Oh it is. I do all types of assessments for client companies.

Mark: Like alarm systems?

Jim: Yeah sure, all the time.

Mark: I think that's fascinating. You must deal with large firms, security and alarm systems being so costly.

Jim: Actually, you'd be surprised.

Mark: Really, I thought a system like that would always be beyond my reach.

Jim: Oh no. In fact, you could install a very good system these days for as little as $8,000.

Mark: $8,000! That's still expensive.

Jim: Well, every firm has its margins. But you know. There are companies that'll shave down their margin considerably just to move their systems: Mine included!

Mark: What do you mean?

Jim: Well, Think about where the money goes. The hardware itself isn't that expensive once it's mass-produced – say one third of the cost. The rest is overhead and labor, and not much for that either. And, since the sales reps almost always work at home, half the price is profit!

Mark: Wow. I just must be living in the clouds thinking that all these great technologies are beyond my reach.

In the end, Mark learned a great deal about Jim's business, especially the information on margin's and how much is profit, and how much is overhead. He's now able to negotiate with much greater knowledge than before. He did this using naïveté as a tool to prompt Jim for information. Jim probably never suspected that Mark was interested in an alarm system based on the discussions. Mark just played it "dumb", but dumb in the sense that he had a reason to be interested, i.e. he had always foregone the installation of an alarm system, because it was thought to be too expensive. Jim, maybe sensing an opportunity to convince Mark otherwise, provided him a wealth of useful information.

Restatement

The restatement technique is a simple means of focusing your contact's attention on key words or phrases that he himself had just uttered, to highlight your interest in his words and to allow him to elaborate on what he'd just stated. The way you do this is to select the word or phrase you'd like to highlight. At a convenient pause in the conversation, you restate that word or phrase to your contact. You may also include an additional prompt, such as a question mark, an inquisitive inflection in your voice, or a word, to demonstrate your interest.

As with all of our techniques, following up your use of restatement with a healthy, silent pause will increase the tendency in your contact to provide elaboration on what he'd just said.

Examples

In this example, Harry is conversing with Will about an attempt by the Harris Brothers to draw Johnson into a business alliance. After Will makes his statement, Harry chooses to prompt Will to talk more about the nature of the alliance. He uses the restatement technique to focus Will on that aspect of the topic, and Will responds.

Will: **"I remember the Harris Brothers were very interested in convincing Johnson to either join the strategic alliance or sell his company."**

Harry: **"Strategic alliance...hmmm..."**

Will: **"Yeah, they were trying to establish a business alliance oriented toward taking over the market..."**

Harry: **" Taking over... hmmm. I think you're referring to the foreign market..."**

Will: **"No, the domestic market. They were looking to put Johnson out of business any way they could."**

In this example, Mary is conducting a job interview and uses the restatement technique to prompt Lawrence to elaborate on his penchant for crime reporting in his previous employment.

Mary: **"So, Lawrence, let's begin with your previous employment. Tell me about where you worked and the responsibilities you had."**

Lawrence: **"Alright. From 1995 to 2002, I worked for Harley Communications. I was a cub reporter at first, as I was straight out of school. I did mainly obituaries the first year, but was**

assigned two high profile murders late in the year."

Mary: "Murders..."

Lawrence: "Yeah, it sounds kind of morbid, but writing those stories really helped me appreciate the emotional connection the people had with the news. It also helped me develop a wide range of sources in law enforcement.

Mary: "Sources in law enforcement?"

Lawrence: "Yeah, you know, I had to cultivate contacts with several detectives, the public information officers, and one or two patrol officers."

Mary: "It sounds like you enjoyed that work."

Lawrence: " I thrived on it. Those stories made me a regular on the crime beat. ...Been at it ever since."

Mary: "Ever since..."

Lawrence: "I kind of specialized in crime reporting...found out I was a natural at it."

Disbelief

The disbelief technique is a simple maneuver intended to prompt your contact to provide more information on a topic by questioning the accuracy, validity or veracity of his statements. Most people believe in what they do, their research, their training concepts, their business models, or professional techniques. When called into question, they will tend to defend themselves by providing a stronger, more persuasive argument, even more detailed supporting data.

In using the disbelief technique, you call into question your contact's statement with an adverse reaction or criticism. You should exercise caution not to criticize your contact too harshly or too emotionally as this could damage the relationship. You might consider citing a third person as the source of the criticism. Alternatively, you could tinge your disbelief with naïveté, playing on the tendencies in your contact to rebut your criticism and to help you learn more about his statement.

Examples

In this example, Anna chooses to employ a provocative statement combined with disbelief based on publicly available information.

Anna: "You know Jim, I find it fascinating that you guys claim to have developed such a definitive HIV drug. So many researchers have been working on this for so long without success that it just seems strange to me you

could have come up with the solution so quickly."

Jim: "I can understand how you feel about our rapid success, but I assure you we've done our homework. In fact, prior to the laboratory research, we spent three years researching what had already been done outside our firm. We've always felt on solid ground and our in house research has now borne that out."

Anna: "Come on! What about clinical trials? You haven't even launched them yet, but you're so confident you've found the cure!"

Jim: "Well that part is true. We're confident the trials will be successful. But honestly it's all based on lab research thus far."

In this example, Marie uses outright disbelief twice to prompt Laurie to discuss further what she knows about Alpha's video game production costs.

Laurie: "What I've heard indicates Alpha Company will be able to develop the new software package for about $9,000,000, and produce it for $5.00 per unit. If they produce 1 million units, as we expect, and sell them for $50.00 per unit, they'll have a per unit profit of $36.00."

Marie: "That's outrageous! You mean to tell me that the $50 game cartridge I buy for my son's video game only costs them $14.00 to produce and market!"

Laurie: "Yeah, that's right."

Marie: "That just can't be!"

Laurie: "It sure is and I'll tell you why. They outsource the code writing to India where the labor costs are very low. There's no more dependence on Silicon Valley programmers. All that code is transmitted over the web at almost no cost! Burning and packaging is all that remains, and that's not expensive when you buy discs and packaging in bulk."

Marie: "Wow, I guess I just never realized how the industry really made such huge profits."

Laurie: "It's all about ridiculously cheap labor and economies of scale. And, oh...don't forget how hooked our kids are on all these games!"

Conversational Layering

Citation/Conversational Layering is a technique you employ to prompt your contact for a specific comment on a specific issue. The way this works is that you initially lead carefully into specific areas by first citing a reputable source with a preparatory statement. This could be a book, a newspaper or journal article, a respected expert, or a news event. The key is that the fact not be challenged, that it comes from an undisputed source. Your objective is to develop the basis for the conversational topic that is agreed upon by both you and your interlocutor. For this reason, having a credible third party source is best. (Note that the information does not have to be indisputable. It simply must exist, i.e. you and your contact it was written. In fact, an article that presents information which prompts disagreement is a perfect tool for prompting your contact to reveal what he knows and feels.)

Next, you comment on how that source impacts you as an individual. You essentially take a statement on a broad topic and bring it "down to earth" by showing your contact that the matter affects you. Your commentary may allow for alternative points of view. The natural flow of the conversation will then permit your contact to respond in kind with information and/or comments on how he is affected by the initial statement.

Finally, you prompt your contact to provide more information or thoughts or with a comment or question. This can take the form of a request for his opinion on the issue, a request for clarification of the issue, a simple request for information, or a comment, which elicits a detailed response.

(Remember that when you choose to ask a question, try phrasing it as a divergent or open question, rather than a leading question. The last thing you want to do is ruin all the hard work you've done to lead your contact into the discussion by asking a leading question, which elicits a simple yes/no response.)

Example
Here is an example of conversational layering in which Tom leads Jason through an explanation of an article he had recently read. Next he comments on how it touches on him, and then uses a comment to smoothly transition Jason into talking about how the issue affects him.

Tom: "I was reading an article the other day in the Journal of Pharmaceutical Marketing, which discussed Gamma Medical's new strategy for distributing their new class of anti-inflammatory drugs directly through physicians to patients. The corporation's VP for marketing commented in the article that Gamma expects to be able to double its gross sales volume using this method. They also expect this will place them in a position of getting their drugs to customers before doctors have the chance to consider other products, thereby increasing overall share of market as well. (Preparatory Statement) Did you see that article?"

Jason: "No, I did not, but I had heard somebody else discussing that very subject the other day. It's a very interesting. There is really no clear way to know whether Gamma's strategy will work or not."

Tom: "I agree. While I'm not an expert in the field, their concept sounds intriguing, but runs the risk of running into opposition from pharmacies and pharmacists' associations." (Commentary)

Jason: "You're probably right. They're not an easy group of firms and professionals to deal with. They've even had a history of troubles with some of the associations. When I worked for them, we had similar troubles."

Tom: "Interesting. Then you must have a fair idea about what the outcome of Gamma's efforts to launch their new distribution campaign will be." (Comment intended to seek an informational response.)

Jason: "Well, first, I believe they will…"

Quid Pro Quo

> "Quid pro quo, Clarice. I tell you things, you tell me things. Not about this case, of course, but about yourself. Quid pro quo. Yes or no, Clarice?"
>
> -Dr. Hannibal Lecter,
> The Silence of the Lambs

The quid pro quo technique is rooted in the human tendency to reciprocate. When we receive something from another person, such as a gift, or an invitation, or some other consideration or kindness, we tend to feel an obligation to reciprocate.

As an elicitation technique, the quid pro quo plays on this tendency in your contact to reciprocate in kind when you offer something. Your offering can be a revelation or admission of a personal nature, if you want to learn about your contact. It can be a useful snippet of professional information, if that's what you want to collect. It can be a complaint or criticism about someone or something.

Examples

In this example of the quid pro quo technique, Karen works to exploit the human tendency to complain. As she senses Martin's frustration, she anticipates his complaint, injecting a comment about her own, similar experience. Martin then responds in similar fashion with his own complaint.

Martin: "I'm feeling a bit underappreciated at work right now. I suppose it'll pass, but I'm not happy about it."

Karen: "I know what you mean. I felt the same way just last week. My boss didn't believe me when I tried to tell him that we were going to have problems servicing our customers while trimming personnel. He didn't listen and it hurt our reputation. You know exactly how I feel."

Martin: "Yes, I do. In fact, I was trying to tell my boss that we would experience a serious downturn in our ability to service customers, if we didn't change our telephone answering services. He just ignored me."

Karen: "I bet that made you feel good. (Tinged with sarcasm) What did you do then?"

Martin: "Well, I tried to take my concerns to her boss..."

Karen: "And she didn't listen..."

Martin: "You got that right! I just got more of the same. You know what it's like! They're the bosses and they know best. They couldn't possibly understand that I'm a recognized expert."

Flattery

> *"Flattery and insults raise the same question: What do you want?"*
>
> -Mason Cooley

> *"Flattery is all right so long as you don't inhale."*
>
> - Adlai E. Stevenson

> *"Flattery is the infantry of negotiation."*
>
> - The Letter of Lord Chandos

These quotes say it all about flattery. Flattery is an effective conversational tool in facilitating your elicitation techniques. Rather than describing it as a technique, we prefer to think of flattery as a conversational lubricant. To the extent your contact is susceptible to hearing good things about him, and we are all susceptible, your use of flattery can enhance rapport building. Just remember that while he likes to be flattered, he also has his own internal sense for the limits. Exceed his perceived limits, and flattery does the relationship more damage than good.

As for its use in elicitation during conversations, recognize that flattery may be used to positively incline your contacts regardless of the specific elicitation techniques you choose to employ.

Example

In this example, Detective Wilson is questioning Mr. Henry Franks, the manager of a local pharmacy, on a recent report he phoned in to the police on a suspicious purchase of peroxide at his store. He uses flattery to attempt to confirm certain aspects of Franks' report.

Wilson: "Sir, could you please explain to me what you saw?"

Franks: "Certainly, detective. The man came into the store like any other customer and grabbed a shopping cart from there." (He points to a neatly organized line of carts.)

Wilson: "And then…"

Franks: "And then, he browsed every aisle from this side of the store to the other."

Wilson: "Is that common – browsing every aisle, I mean?"

Franks: "Oh yeah, often a customer isn't familiar with our layout and literally looks at every aisle to find what he wants."

Wilson: "But, your store is neatly organized, better than others like it."

Franks: "Well, that's why I called. The man was clearly unfamiliar with the layout. He was from outside the area, and he filled the cart with peroxide. I thought that was suspicious."

Wilson: "You're right to think so, sir. Are you always that closely attuned to your customers' behaviors while shopping?"

Franks: "Yes, my staff and I pride ourselves on that. We are always prepared to assist them with their purchases. That's why we're the best store in the region."

Wilson: "You're certainly on top of every detail. Did any of your employees see the man as well, sir?"

Franks: "No, detective. Johnny Adams was in the stock room logging in a shipment of hair products. You're welcome to talk with him. He's here now. But..."

Wilson: "Yes..."

Franks: "You may like to review the security video. We have it cues up for you to view in the stick room."

Sincerity

> "True emotions and sincere words never perish. The great heart of humanity gladly receives and embalms every true utterance of the humblest of its offspring."
>
> - Elias Lyman Magoon
> Dictionary of Burning Words of Brilliant Writers (1895)

Sincerity is a way to approach the relationships you have with people. As long as you remain sincere, open and honest with your contacts, you will build relationships that last. In fact, as that relationship builds, your need to use manipulative elicitation techniques will subside, just as your contact's willingness to share information with you will increase.

Loaded Questions/Comments

The elicitation technique we call the Loaded Questions or Loaded Comment is similar the concept of the presumptive question or bait question in law enforcement interrogations. Essentially, you limit your contact's range of possible responses in an attempt to prompt him to confirm or admit the information you are looking for. Additionally, you may choose to skew your question or comment either positively or negatively to increase your chances of success.

As noted above, this technique is similar to the presumptive question in police interrogation parlance in that you presume something in your comment that may not be valid. You are in essence "fishing" for information or an admission that may never come. The consequences of this are that you may demonstrate a lack of knowledge or information about the topic to your contact and ruin your chances of pursuing the discussion further.

The key to using a loaded question or comment successfully is preparation. If you are going to comment on or ask about the negative aspects of someone's management style, you need to be reasonably certain there are negative aspects. If you want to know how much time a drug smuggler spent in Colombia with the Medellin Cartel, you'd better be reasonably certain he's a drug smuggler. In other words, you've got to collect some background knowledge before proceeding with the question or comment.

Examples

In this real life example, a child innocently asks his mother for something to eat. His question is not, however, as simple as it looks. Almost instinctively, the child seems to know that if he asks, "Mom, may I have something to eat?" he could receive a yes or no response. This means that he stands a chance of receiving nothing to eat. What he does, however, is to ask his mother in effect for a list of the foods he may eat. The mother is naturally predisposed to respond with the least resistance and provides the child a list a foods every time.

"Mom, What can I have to eat?"

In this example, the person asking the question is presuming that the subject of his inquiry performs poorly, and focuses the respondent on this. The respondent, preconditioned by the slant of the question, is more likely to think about the subject's performance in negative terms and provide a response. If the subject does not perform poorly, the respondent will have to overcome the bias in the question to provide an objective response.

"Tell me about his poor performance?"

In this example, the interrogator has presumed that the subject of his interrogation has spent time training in the mountains of Pakistan. If his presumption is reasonably accurate, the subject, suspecting his interrogator knows about his time in Pakistan, is more likely to respond than if the interrogator has to fish for information more broadly. The risk in this example is that if the interrogator is fishing for information and has no knowledge at all of the subject's experiences, he may inadvertently bolster the subject's confidence that he can resist the questions.

> "So, how many weeks did you spend training in the Northwest Frontier Province?"

Asking Permission

> Don: Let me ask you something, not about this.
> David: About Liz?
> Don: Yeah, how did you know?
> David: You asked permission to ask.
>
> - Numb3rs, Tabu

Many times during elicitation efforts you will find yourself on the brink of an interesting opportunity to collect what you need. However, you are concerned that your contact will react negatively or will become reluctant to engage you. Perhaps the topic is too personal, or perhaps it's proprietary. You have two choices. You can back away from the issue and give up the chance to collect what you need. Or you can forge ahead. In forging ahead, you must avoid alienating your contact by being too forward, yet still give yourself a chance to collect the information. But how do you do that?

You ask permission to ask your question.

This may sound awkward, but by asking a simple question of this sort, you accomplish two things. First, you gage your contact's reaction to the topic without alienating him. And second, you show deference to your contact, by giving him the power to engage you on the topic or not. Few people will completely rebuff your efforts, if you defer to them by asking permission first.

Examples
In this example, Mark asks Dave if he could ask about his involvement in developing his firm's research strategy. Dave responds well to the request for permission and volunteers a response.

Mark: "You know, I'm intrigued by you what you'd told me about your firm's research strategy and it brings to mind a question I'd like to ask you, but I feel a little awkward about it.

Dave: "Awkward about what?"

Mark: "Well, I'd really like to talk about the development your long term research strategy."

Dave: "I'd be happy to discuss that with you."

Mark: "Really? That's great! Would you mind if I ask you about how you decided on the product range you did?"

Dave: "No, no. I'd be happy to tell you about that. In fact, it began seven years ago…"

In this example, Dave doesn't respond as positively, but will continue the discussion, as Mark has given him the power to discuss the topic or not. In an attempt to be helpful, he offers to answer other questions Mark may have. Now, you would expect Mark to be disappointed about his first question, and he is. But, that doesn't end this opportunity to elicit from Dave. He uses the opportunity to prompt Dave for comments on Alpha Company, and Dave complies.

Mark: "You know, I'm intrigued by what you'd told me about your firm's research strategy and it brings to mind a question I'd like to ask you. Would you mind if I ask you about how you developed your strategy?"

Dave: "Well, Mark, I can certainly understand your interest in our strategy. Unfortunately, beyond the broad comments I made, we consider our strategy to be proprietary. I would prefer not to comment. Is there anything else you'd like to know?"

Mark: "Well, I appreciate your position. Thanks. As for other issues, what do you think about Alpha Company's research efforts? "

Dave: "Well, Alpha certainly does have a solid strategy. They seem to me to be…"

Disagreement

> *"The beginning of thought is in disagreement, not only with others but also with ourselves."*
> *- Eric Hoffer*

Disagreement as an elicitation technique is similar to the disbelief technique in that you are calling into question the validity of your contact's point of view. In showing your uncertainty of his line of reasoning, you are prompting him to discuss the topic in greater detail by exploiting his tendency to defend him opinion. That greater detail will contain more information.

There are two ways to disagree with your contact. In the first, you disagree directly with him. You state your point of view and hope that he will respond by trying to convince you that his point of view is correct. The challenge in disagreeing in this way is that you are hoping your contact will respond. The worst-case scenario is he will accept that your views differ and leave it at that.

In the second form of disagreement, you point out that somebody else, some third party, disagrees with your contact's point of view. In this use of the technique, you present the dissonant view to your contact and then prompt him to provide support for his own view. This allows him to believe he is convincing you that his view is correct.

Example
    In this example, Karen presents her thoughts on why the weather has been so unpredictable lately. Joan disagrees with her directly, hoping to elicit a more detailed response. Note that this form of disagreement presents limited opportunity for eliciting detailed information.

Karen: "Personally, I believe we've had such unpredictable storms this year, because of sun spot activity. Meteorologists at the university have just published an article on this in the Journal of Weather Sciences."

Joan: "That's really interesting, Karen, but I disagree. I think this is a typical, cyclical period in which we are due to have more storms, more rain and later on more snow. Just look at the historical data."

Karen: "I know. I have reviewed that data myself as well. There are a few things that the data doesn't explain though, like the expanded range of the aurora borealis."

Joan: "I don't see the connection."

Karen: "The connection is plain to see. I'd ask you to read the article. It's really fascinating."

In this second example, David and Paula are discussing militant Islamic terrorism. They each support differing points of view. In this use of the disagreement technique, David expresses a third party's disagreement with Paula's view, thus, providing less disagreement between the two and more opportunity for discussion.

Paula: "I subscribe to the idea that Islamic extremism, the resort to the use of violence, is purely a religious imperative dictated in our age by the involvement of the United States in Middle Eastern affairs."

David: "That's an interesting view, and there's certainly plenty of evidence to suggest that's the case, but I am a bit uncertain."

Paula: "How so?"

David: "Well, Johansson has stated in his recent articles that he believes about the same thing you do, but he also accepts that local political considerations, whether tied to the United States or not, also play a role."

Paula: "I can see your point. Johansson makes a strong point. He tends to believe that dissatisfaction with the local political process explains the rise of extremism."

David: "Yes, you've seen his articles."

Paula: "Oh, yes, I read his work all the time. What he fails to consider is the role played by outside powers. The British role in governing Egypt as an imperial power after World War I contributed to the rise of the Muslim Brotherhood. And I believe the U.S. presence in Saudi Arabia during the First Gulf War contributed to Jihadist desires to wage war on us."

David: "Paula, I don't disagree with you. (In fact, he does...slightly.) The issue is certainly complicated. It's still difficult to grasp the depth of the challenges in the region. There are political leadership issues in every country. There is widespread economic distress, especially amongst the younger age groups. And there's even the issue of artificial borders that divide tribal and ethnic groups contrary to their histories."

Paula: "I accept much of that. The issues are complicated. What I would suggest if that..."

Humor

Humor is an important tool in conversation and elicitation. Jokes, light sarcasm, self-effacing comments and humor tend to relax people and put them more at ease. It reduces tensions and much like flattery renders people more open, more talkative and more likeable. To the extent you can inject humor into your conversations at the right times and in the right amounts, you can relax your contacts rendering them more amenable to your elicitation efforts. If you are not naturally humorous, be cautious at first. Natural, carefully dosed humor is a wonderful part of conversation. Overdone it shuts it down before it starts.

Silence

> *"We fill the silence with our own insecurities."*
>
> *- Eddie Arlette, "Keen Eddie"*

'Silence is Golden.' We've all heard this proverb since we were children. It's been around forever, or at least it seems like it has. And it will probably stay with us forever, because there are small gold nuggets of truth in it. And one of those nuggets is that if you wait before you speak and give your contact time, you'll usually be rewarded with something you did not already know, i.e. new information. The key is to resist the temptation to continually fill the silence with talk. Allowing silence essentially pressures your contact, rather than you, to fill that void.

Looked at in these terms, silence is not only an elicitation technique, but also the perfect accompaniment to all elicitation techniques. Learning to time the use of silence can be a significant advantage in prompting your contacts to provide you volumes of information.

There is another useful aspect of silence as referenced in character Eddie Arlette's quote from the television series Keen Eddie; "We fill the silence with our own insecurities." In interviews and interrogations, silence focuses people inward on their own thoughts and actions. This is particularly true of those who feel guilt. When confronted with long silences in conversations, they often provide clues to what they thinking in their responses to you. These are excellent opportunities to get to know your contacts better and better.

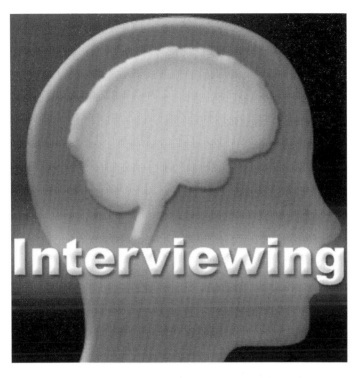

The Human Skills: Interviewing

By Frank Stopa

The Human Skills: Interviewing

Contents

What is an Interview?

Webster's New Collegiate Dictionary defines an interview as "a meeting at which information is obtained ... from a person." In practical terms, an interview is an interpersonal interaction in which you, the interviewer, collect information from another person, your contact, through the employment of a variety of techniques. These techniques include various types of questions, elicitation techniques, and other Human Skills Techniques.

In addition to simply collecting information through the employment of a variety of techniques, we should keep in mind that your contact's willingness to engage you, as well as the degree of control you may have over the circumstances of the interview would vary widely depending on the nature of your interview.

Willing Contact or Not?

Your contact would at first blush seem to be a willing participant in your interview. Consider, however, that an interview can be many things. It can be an interview by the FBI to investigate a crime. It can be a visa interview to convince a consular officer to issue a visa. It can be a job interview. It can be an investigative journalist's efforts to get to the bottom of a story in the news. It can be a magazine or television interview. It can be an interview of an industry analyst to obtain competitor insights.

Given these different scenarios, you may experience vastly differing degrees of willingness on the part of your contact to reply to your questions. Each contact has different motivations. Some submit willingly your questions, while others have no choice. Your assessment of the motivations and willingness of your contact will have a strong impact upon how you maximize the collection of information.

Control Over Circumstances

Just as there will be a wide range of willingness in your contacts, you will also have to cope with varying degrees of control over the circumstances or setting of the interview. Job interviews tend to be controlled by the interviewing organization and take place in their offices. The applicant typically has little to no control. If you are the interviewer, you may be able to exercise considerable power over the job seeker. Law enforcement interviews can be awkward and uncomfortable. If you are the investigating officer, you may be trying to extract a criminal confession: not usually an easy task. If you are the suspect, you are either being asked to provide evidence or prompted to confess to the crime. You may even find yourself in a jail cell answering questions. A media interview may grow uncomfortable for the interviewee as difficult topics are broached. This can become uncomfortable for both the interviewer and interviewee. Interviews of industry analysts can fit anywhere in between.

Core Concepts of Interviewing

The Information Collection Spectrum

     The Information Collection Spectrum describes a continuum of human source information collection activities, which share a variety of techniques and concepts. They are at their foundations similar in that they all share the objective of prompting your contact to provide information. What differentiates them, one from another, are the degree of control you exercise over the interaction with your contact, including the setting, and the degree of willingness displayed by your contact to comply with your agenda, hidden or not.

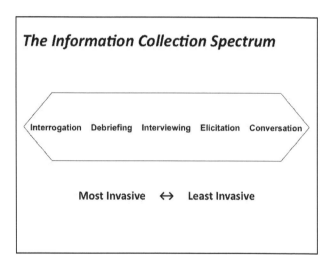

Interrogation
     Interrogation is most often considered a military, intelligence or law enforcement tool intended to

prompt a suspect to provide intelligence information or evidence. The interrogator typically exercises control over the setting of the interrogation, as well as the direction of the questioning. We often envision interrogation as a hostile activity in which the suspect displays disdain for the interrogator and an unwillingness to provide information. Although many information collection techniques may be applied to interrogations, simple question and answer forms the its basis.

Debriefing

Debriefing is the act of asking questions of another person to obtain useful information. Debriefing is often considered a military or intelligence tool employed in collecting battlefield or political intelligence from a soldier or a confidential informant, although similar activities take place in other fields as well. The debriefer often exercises control over the setting as well as the direction of the questioning. The soldier, informant, or other contact, is typically a willing interlocutor.

Interviewing

Interviewing covers a wide range of information collection activities, including journalistic and media interviews, job interviews, and police interviews of witnesses. The interviewer generally maintains control over the direction of the interview, although this depends to an extent on the willingness of the contact. The contact may be a job applicant willing to share any information that helps him obtain employment, or somebody resisting an overly inquisitive journalist. As for the setting, either party may influence or control where the interview takes place.

Elicitation

Elicitation may be thought of as 'conversation with an agenda.' We can characterize it as an information collection effort in which the elicitor attempts to exercise control over the direction of the conversation without revealing his agenda to his contact. As for setting, a wide range of influence may be exercised by either party as to where they converse. And finally, there may be a wide range of willingness in the contact to providing information at the elicitor's prompting.

Conversation

A conversation is an activity in which two people talk, exchange information willingly and typically do not have any initial information collection agendas. Either side may choose to suggest a setting. Both sides typically converse more or less freely, and the conversation meanders with no apparent objective.

The Planning Cycle

The planning cycle is our simple method for assuring you maximize your information collection. First you Prepare & Plan your interview, then you Act, in other words, you conduct the interview and collect the information you're seeking, and then you Review & Record your results.

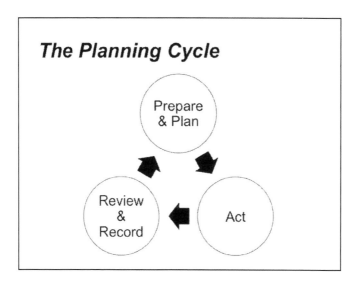

Prepare & Plan

This phase of the Planning Cycle is all about getting yourself ready to interview your contact.

Know Your Objective

Knowing what information or what kind of information you want to collect is the first step in determining how to go about collecting that information. This does not mean you must know exactly what information you'll obtain, but it does mean you should know what kind of result you are looking for.

Know Your Contact

People are generally more willing to engage you, if they feel at ease in your company. When you know something about your contact in advance, you have gotten over the first hurdle. The benefits of doing this should never be underestimated. This part of learning about your contact is actually the beginning of building a long-lasting relationship. As you'll see later on, we recommend you learn as much as you can about your contact's personality. The following questions will help you understand the kinds of things you might like to know.

Has your contact written anything that will help you understand his personality, beliefs, ideals, etc.?
Do you have a photograph?
What is his age?
What is his age relative to you?
What are his political views?
What are his personal likes/dislikes?
Does he prefer casual or more formal dress?
Is he married? Does he have children?

Organize Your Approach

Conversations can be unpredictable, usually taking you in unexpected directions. Preparing an agenda will assist you in making sense of those unexpected directions, quickly allowing you to determine what information you have collected and what opportunity or potential remains in the conversation. We recommend you prepare notes and questions. Even if you can't use them during your conversation, writing them down will permit you to assimilate them, to have that information at your disposal when it counts most.

Practice

To the extent possible, we recommend you review your notes, rehearse your questions, and anticipate your contact's reactions. There is a saying in war, that "no plan survives contact with the enemy." The same is true of any activity based on human interaction; your conversations will never play out as you had envisioned. If you've made an honest attempt to anticipate the unexpected, you will be better prepared to handle it when things don't play out as planned.

Act

This is the interview or conversation during which you carry out your information collection. It is during this phase of the Planning Cycle that you will reconfirm what you know, or don't know, about your contact; apply the Core Concepts of Interviewing we will examine in the next chapter to understand how to maximize your information collection, and employ our interviewing techniques that will allow you to collect the information you want.

Review & Record

We believe strongly that you should review your results immediately, document them in some way, and then plan for next opportunity. Your interview will undoubtedly include moments for which you were able to plan your actions to maximize the collection of information. This will result in a wide range of experiences as well as results. Reviewing those experiences and results, and documenting them, will develop in you a sense of strategy to your efforts. You will begin collecting bits and pieces of information from various contacts, which together form a comprehensive picture. You will also being to learn valuable lessons about your own interviewing skills, which will help you improve. The following questions may help you review your encounters.

What did you learn about your contact?
How does it compare with what I already know?
What will you try to learn about him the next time?
What did you learn from your contact?
How does it compare with what I already know?
What did you NOT learn or collect?

> What will you attempt to learn the next time?

Recording your results is every bit as important as reviewing them. With the amounts of information we deal with every day and the way we network constantly, meeting new people both face to face and virtually, it is becoming more and more difficult to keep everything organized in our minds. Therefore, documenting your results in some way is almost an imperative. Now, this doesn't mean you have to create a 'dossier' on everyone you meet. What it does mean is you should take advantage of some of the various address book and contacts applications that all of our smart phones and laptops make available to us.

Finally, it is worth mentioning that the benefit of reviewing and recording your results is that you can quickly compare those results against your collection agenda. This allows you to more easily plan what and how to obtain the remaining information. Planning for the next collection opportunity brings you full circle in the Planning Cycle.

The Structured Interview

The Structured Interview is less an actual structure for conducting an interview or than it is a general guide to the flow most human interaction follows. While no two human interactions are ever the same, most do share some basic characteristics. These include the greeting, the actual interaction and the closing. Since we are specifically looking at interactions during which you are attempting to collect information, we have chosen to extend the interaction portion into three steps, which we will call Listening, Asking and the Recap.

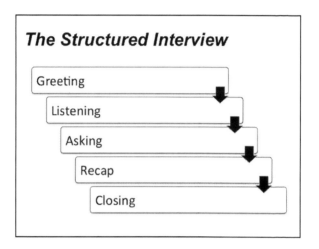

The Structured Interview

Greeting

Listening

Asking

Recap

Closing

Greeting

The Greeting is the opening phase of the conversation. As you might surmise, it's all about putting your contact at ease and setting the stage to collect information. The greeting begins quite literally with the greeting, welcoming you contact, exchanging pleasantries and building rapport. The goal is to put your contact at ease, because when people feel comfortable, they are much more amenable to sharing information.

The greeting concludes with setting the stage for your information collection agenda. This entails explaining your interests. In a friendly conversation, this might be nothing more than expressing your desire to enjoy your contact's company. In a police interrogation it might entail explaining much more blatantly your objective of determining the suspect's guilt or innocence. The key here is to gently channel your contact into the frame of mind in which he is predisposed to provide you information.

Finally, please keep in mind that the Greeting can be a short exchange of "hello's", it can be a curt business-like handshake, or it can be an hour-long procession through rapport building and re-establishing relationships that is common in other parts of the world. Whichever end of the spectrum you come from, you can't avoid the Greeting. Make the most of it.

Listening

The next phase of the conversation is what we call Listening. This is when you allow your contact to have the attention. Nobody likes being 'talked at'. People prefer to be able to express themselves. While you may be trying to collect specific kinds of information, there will often be times when your contact will open your eyes to new information, or a new perspective on your subject. Let that happen, you can always return later to your agenda items.

The bottom line is you'll never know what you don't know, unless you ask. Another benefit this has for your interview is the way seeking input from your contact helps achieve a degree of "buy in" to your agenda. In other words, if he feels like you are making him feel important enough to be consulted during the interview, he will likely work harder in identifying the information that matters most to you.

Asking

This now brings you to the pursuit of your information collection agenda. Once you've set the stage for your interview or debriefing, this is when you actually collect the information you need. Here, you manage the conversation to take on topics of interest to you that help satisfy your collection agenda. It is here in the contact that you employ your interviewing techniques to fine-tune your collection effort.

Recap

Your penultimate step emphasizes the need to review the work you have done with your contact. This is intended to assure that you have collected the information correctly. One truth about collecting information your contact is that its transmission is often subject to your perceptions of what your contact provided. If you've ever played a word game in which people pass on a story from one person to the next until the last person is asked to repeat the story and discover how it has changed, then you know how even the simplest information can be distorted through passage from one person to another. Reviewing what you have collected with your contact ensures that you have correctly perceived it. It is in this stage that you can correct mistakes in specific pieces of information, ensure your understanding of the facts, and account for differences in perception of that information between you and your contact.

Closing

      Finally, we come to the close of the meeting. This is when you thank your contact for taking the time to meet with you. But this is not all that you do. You also continue to develop rapport and lay the groundwork for future meetings. Anybody who works with people on a regular basis knows the importance of building a relationship. You just never know when you'll need to ask a contact, friend or acquaintance for a favor, or for information. You'll never know when the friendly relationship you built will pay off in terms of a sale. You'll never know when you will need to or want to call on your contact for more information. Do yourself a favor. Don't alienate your interlocutor, always leave the possibility for future contact open - it may pay dividends some day.

Active Listening

      It is said that 60% of problems that between people and within businesses are communications problems. Madelyn Burley-Allen, in her book Listening, The Forgotten Skill, asserts that 40% of the time spent in interpersonal communication is spent listening. This means that 24% of all interpersonal communications problems can be thought of as being problems in listening.

      That's almost 25%! That means that where your inability to close deals, make sales, reach mutually beneficial negotiating outcomes, overcome internal personnel management problems, transfer and share human knowledge, collect information and develop a competitive advantage, and more, could be improved by almost 25%!

Can you imagine the added value you would bring to your business if you could reduce that percentage to say 15%? How about 10%? What's that worth to your bottom line? As you can see, listening effectively is critical to improving your performance.

The amazing thing about listening is that it is not difficult to improve your ability. All you need to do is follow a few simple guidelines and develop good listening habits. Over time you will notice that you learn more about and from your contacts.

What is involved in Listening?

Let's look at three basic components of active listening. These are Comprehension, Evaluation, and Response.

Comprehension is the act of understanding the message that the speaker wishes to impart. The understanding of a given piece of information depends upon the perceptions you bring to the conversation. To the extent they are the same as the speaker's perceptions, you will correctly comprehend the meaning. To the extent you have developed knowledge of your contact, as well as built a relationship with him, you will understand better and better those basic perceptions that impact the meaning of a particular piece of information.

Another aspect of comprehension is listening to non-verbal signals. Non-verbal signals can be as important as verbal responses. If you've ever noticed the physical reactions people have when you converse with them, you know what we are talking about. When people listen to you and absorb what you have to say, they are usually more relaxed. They show greater interest. They are often more personable and open to your suggestions. They face you directly. They make more frequent eye contact. On the other hand, those who do not listen do not make eye contact. They 'close' their bodies. They might cross their arms and legs. They may not face you directly. They may be tense and resistant to cooperation and collaboration. They are less personable, and do not seem to have an interest in what you're saying.

Evaluation is the next activity in active listening. Evaluation is the process of determining whether or not the message the speaker imparted fulfills your objectives. In other words, are you collecting the information you wanted to collect? Is the information relevant to the interview or debriefing? Does it add anything new to what you already know? If it does not respond to your question, or doesn't add anything new, what exactly is the response? What information is was imparted? Answering these questions for yourself as you proceed through a conversation is important in determining whether or not you are meeting your information collection objectives.

Finally, we move on to Response. Response is the act of demonstrating that you are actively engaged in the communication. It involves showing interest in the information, as well as interest in the effort made by the speaker to provide you that information. This not only requires your silence to display that you are listening. It also requires verbal and non-verbal responses to the speaker to prove that you are engaged. If you omit these responses, your contact will soon perceive that you are disinterested and lose interest himself. Once he's lost interest, you don't get any more information!

Questions to Keep in Mind as You Listen
If you keep the following questions in mind during your interviews, you will assure you comprehend and are properly evaluating what you hear.

Is it clear to me what the response means?
What exactly is my contact saying?
Is the information relevant to my question?
Is the response complete?
Does the tone of voice carry any meaning or significance?
How does my contact feel about the response?
Is the response really the truth?
Should I interrupt now or wait until later?

Other Effective Listening Techniques

Don't Interrupt

Have you ever been on the verge of getting a thought out in a conversation when somebody cuts you off? Did you feel like he curtailed your thought, because he probably didn't care about what you were saying? Of course you did. More than likely, he wasn't really listening to you as much as he was thinking about what he wanted to say.

When you're on the listening end of a conversation allow your contact to get through what he wants to say. You might be surprised by the information you obtain. Allowing him to complete his thoughts also gives you the time to formulate better questions. You also send the non-verbal message that you are genuinely interested in what he has to say.

Clarifiers

Clarifying questions, comments or prompts are valuable in two ways. First, they help you assure you understand what your contact is saying. And second, they serve as positive responses to your contact, i.e. that you are listening and are interested. Repeat your contact's key words (see the restatement technique) or rephrase them in your own words to assure he was heard and understood. Clarifiers may also be used to prompt your contact for more detail.

"Let me see if I understand…"
"If I understand correctly, what you're saying is…"

"I'm intrigued. Tell me more about…"
"I'm confused, does that mean…"
"That's interesting. Would you explain the background to that?"
"Right. And what would the implications of that be for…?"

Put Your Ego to the Side

Most people like those who listen to them. Understanding this is another important lesson you can learn about improving your listening skills. This is because most people want to be the center of attention and actively pursue that attention. This stems from a basic desire to be liked, appreciated, and understood. Think about instances when somebody interrupted you. More than likely they were succumbing to the natural urge to seek attention. Most people don't even realize they're doing it. In fact, we all do it from time to time.

If your goal were to collect information from your contact, it would be counterproductive to compete with each other for the other's attention. When you compete for attention communication falters and information ceases to flow. The next time you are conversing with a friend, try NOT to seek his attention. Allow him to win yours. You'll be rewarded for your efforts.

Special Considerations

Information collection from human sources doesn't always occur in face-to-face meetings. With the increasing use of technology to communicate, your interactions may also take place via cell phone, e-mail, or even text messaging. Although filtered through tech devices and conducted over the bridges of time and distance, these interactions are still human interactions. These situations present challenges that must be factored into your planning.

You must still develop rapport, build a relationship and listen as actively as possible, i.e. it's all about the relationship. It's no different in cell phone conversations, e-mail and texting. It's simply more challenging.

The Lack of Feedback

The largest problem with conducting an interview over the phone, via e-mail or text messaging is the paucity of non-verbal signals from your contact. In 1971 in his book Silent Messages, UCLA Professor Albert Mehrabian, PhD discovered through his research on non-verbal communication that only about 7% of all emotional communication between people was actually communicated through the spoken word. The largest percentage of communication was affected through the passage of information in the form of body language, as much as 55%, and the tone or inflection of the voice, as much as 38%. In other words, as much as 93% of information related to emotions communicated between two people does NOT come in the form of verbal communication.

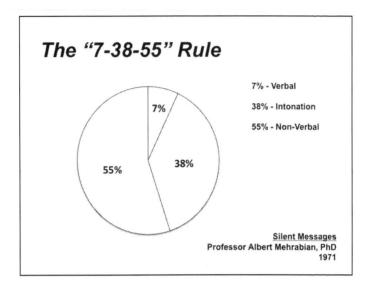

The "7-38-55" Rule

7% - Verbal

38% - Intonation

55% - Non-Verbal

Silent Messages
Professor Albert Mehrabian, PhD
1971

On the telephone, you can hear your interviewee talk and you can hear the tome of his voice, but you are unable to collect the information normally available in the body language, facial expressions, and gestures. This can reduce your collection of sensory information by as much as 55%.

Via e-mail and text messaging, you face an even more daunting problem. In addition to the absence of body language, facial expressions and gestures, you can't hear your contact in real time. You can only read. Now you may have just eliminated as much as 38% of the information upon which you rely to develop a complete sense for the substantive information you are collecting and your contact's reaction to your agenda and interests.

120

Again, that's an absence of as much as 93% of the information that might be available to you in a face-to-face interview. Given these limitations, how do you improve your chances of effectively collecting and communicating information via impersonal communication? We have several suggestions.

- **Determine Clear Objectives**
- **Carefully Plan and Structure**
- **Pay Attention to Non-Verbal Signals**

Determine Clear Objectives

Determining how you are going to use phone, e-mail or texting for your interview is the critical first step in using that means of communications effectively. Toward this end, ask yourself the following questions.

1. Do you need to collect substantive information via impersonal means?

There are certainly times when you will not be able to meet face-to-face with your contact. If you need information quickly and can obtain it via phone, e-mail or texting, you may not have to schedule a personal meeting. Personal meetings may be impossible given time and geographic constraints. Or you may be involved in telemarketing activities or phone/e-mail surveys, and do not desire more than an impersonal response from your contact. In other words, determine the constraints you have on arranging face-to-face meetings, as well as whether a face-to-face meeting is required.

2. Is there time sensitivity to your interview?

There are times when you need fast responses to your questions. This happens all the time. Can you afford to wait until the next face-to-face? If not, you may have to plan your interview to include impersonal communications.

3. Are face-to-face meetings impossible?

Maybe you are communicating with a contact living in another part of the world. You can't easily see each other due to the cost of travel, or the time needed to get there. In this case, you may have to rely on less personal communications to conduct your interview.

4. Will the impersonal side of your interview be used to supplement face-to-face interviewing?

Maybe you already meet your contact regularly and communicate impersonally. In these cases, you may wish to supplement your collection via less personal collection.

Carefully Plan and Structure

As we have said earlier, one of the real downsides to using less personal means of communications with your contact is that it requires greater structure in preparing and planning the contact than do face-to-face meetings. This is due to the greatly reduced availability of sensory input, not to mention the reduced time to collect what you need. However, You can turn this to your advantage through better planning and preparation. Additionally, you can control when you make the phone call, or send the e-mail or text message.

Keep in mind as well that over the phone, you will likely find your contact in the midst of other activity. Realistically, you are interrupting him. He will accord you time to accomplish your interview, but the fact is that even if you have pre-scheduled a phone call, you will still likely be an intrusion.

In e-mail or other impersonal contact, you run into similar problems. These, however, are a function of time more than interruption. Busy people simply do not have time to read long, detailed questionnaires, memos or notes. This becomes an even more acute problem when you talk to people who are more and more senior in their fields. They are typically so busy with their own affairs that they have little time to actually read the detailed documents that cross their desks. The solution to this is to plan your e-mail messages, documents, and letters in ways that provide the needed information without excessive length. Consider organizing your emails to include the following:

- **Information Bullets**
- **Graphs and Charts**
- **Multiple Choice Questions**
- **Concise Sentences**
- **Reduced Verbiage**

Pay Attention to Non-Verbal Signals

Finally, keep in mind that when you use impersonal means of communications you might consider paying more attention to the non-verbal signals in your contacts' words. These signals are still there, although they are much tougher to identify. Take greater care in interpreting and acting upon those signals. In telephone conversations, you are able to get a better sense for non-verbal signals, because you can hear the tone of your interlocutor's voice. In e-mail and text messaging, this is non-existent.

Be careful of relying too much on your sense of humor, satire, disbelief, etc. All of these are much more difficult to interpret in your written or printed word, just as they are in interpreting your contacts' written or printed words. There are several things that you may keep in mind to avoid problems in interpreting non-verbal signals in phone, e-mail/written communications. They are:

- **Take time to understand your contact's personality before the communication takes place – obviously having had a face-to-face meeting before hand is of immense value.**

- **Remain alert to the presence of non-verbal signals.**

- **Don't act on any non-verbal signals unless/until you are confident that you understand the context in which they were sent.**

Interviewing Techniques

In this chapter we will look at a series of specific techniques for asking questions of, and dealing with, your subjects. When used in conjunction with the concepts you have already learned, you will improve your ability to collect better, more detailed information from virtually any interview. These techniques will also serve as the foundation upon which you can also build other information collection skills.

Choosing Vocabulary

Your choice of vocabulary is an important consideration in achieving your information collection objectives and should be:

- **Clear and Understandable Vocabulary**
- **Vocabulary Specific to the Field**
- **Vocabulary that Does Not Inadvertently Prompt a False Response**

Clear and Understandable Vocabulary

In formulating questions, you should assure your subject understands your vocabulary. Your word selection should match the educational level, age, and socio-economic strata, of your subject. In most cases, you we would advise you to adhere to the 'KISS' principle, 'keep it simple, stupid', because you may never know the exact intellectual level of your subject. Starting with good, simple and understandable vocabulary will assure every subject understands you. As you become accustomed to your subject, you can employ simpler or more complicated language.

Examples of Clear and Understandable Vocabulary

In this first example, Laura's poor choice of vocabulary obscures her intent and leads Barbara to misunderstand her question.

Laura	"Barbara, Lloyd asked me yesterday to look into expenditures in the office and I was pleased he asked me, because I think we're spending too much on office supplies. I'd like to ask you about how much you team spends per month, because I think you guys are the most frugal, but I have to figure out who spends most. Can you do that for me?"
Barbara	"What?"

Now, this example is much better. Laura's choice of vocabulary reflects that she is aware of the concepts and issues in Barbara's work. As a result, Barbara responds more easily and with more detail.

Laura	"Barbara, Lloyd has asked me to look at office expenditures on supplies. I'd like to ask about your team's expenses. Is that alright?"
Barbara	"Sure, what do you need?"
Laura	"Do you have a spread sheet with monthly supply purchases?"

Barbara	"I sure do. I'll send it to you."
Laura	"Great! Thank you. By the way, Lloyd wants to use your team as an example of our best practices. Would that be alright?"
Barbara	"Sure, as long as you don't overemphasize us. We have to work with the other teams on a daily basis."

Specific Vocabulary

Specific vocabulary can be important in establishing the correct level of expertise between you and your subject. You want to have the necessary vocabulary at your command, especially if you work within a specific field. In this instance your credibility will likely be accepted and responses to your questions will typically contain more detail.

However, if you are not an expert, you want to use just enough specific vocabulary to display that you understand the scope of the issues at hand. You should not pretend to be more than you are; a true expert will see through you in a few moments. The key to choosing vocabulary in this case is to know the basic vocabulary of the subject, and to understand some of the basics of the field. You should readily admit that you have done your homework, but are not an expert. More often than not, this will tell your subject that you are serious. This will also allow you to ask your interlocutor for assistance in understanding the details of the issue.

As we have talked about in the section on building the relationship, this is akin to "playing the student." It helps build rapport, and places you in the proper "professor-student" relationship with your interlocutor to permit him/her to provide knowledge to you.

Example of Specific Vocabulary

The first example is one in which the interviewer doesn't really understand the subject area he is asking about, nuclear reactor operations. The first question will evoke a response that will likely contain less detail and may prompt the respondent to teach the interviewer the basics of nuclear power. This might detract from the actual information he might impart.

The second example of choosing vocabulary specific to nuclear power demonstrates to your contact that you have read something about his field and can intelligently ask questions.

"After you burn the fuel in the reactor and make electricity, what happens to the radioactive waste? Can it explode?"

"Once you have irradiated the fissionable material in the reactor core, converted the released energy into steam to operate the turbines, and produced electricity, how do you separate out the fission by products so as to render them safe for disposal?"

Inadvertently Prompting False Responses

You should be aware that the use of certain types of vocabulary might inadvertently lead your interlocutor to provide false or inaccurate responses. This is not because he/she is knowingly providing false information, but because you may be injecting subtle hints into your questions that affect the responses. Just as criticism can adversely affect the development of rapport, and pre-judging a response can impair your listening skills, injecting words with negative or positive connotations could lead your interlocutor to provide a response he/she might believe you are looking for. These produce what we call "loaded questions." We will examine them later in this section, as well as in our look at elicitation. However, in terms of vocabulary use, you can avoid false responses by staying away from positive or negatively tinged words in your questions.

Avoid wording your questions with positive or negative connotations.

Once you have used a more neutral question to narrow down the range of possible responses, then you can proceed into more subjective examinations of your interlocutor's responses. For instance, in our salesperson example, once you have determined what factors contribute to the salesperson's performance, you can then delve into whether or not they contributed to success or failure. If you start off with the first question, you have already framed out the discussion, i.e. 'the salesperson is the best.' This may not necessarily be an opinion shared by your interlocutor and might negatively impact the kinds of responses you receive. Your interlocutor may choose to rebut your description of the salesperson as one of the best, and not provide objective information on what contributes to his performance. Or, he may presume that the salesperson is the best, based upon what you have asked, and provide you speculation as to why this might be the case. In neither instance are you collecting objective information. Removing positive and negative connotations in the initial phases of a debriefing and/or interview will help you avoid this problem.

Examples of Inadvertently False Responses
In constructing your questions, try to eliminate the possibility of prompting your contact to unknowingly provide false or biased responses.

Do	Don't
"In your opinion, what are the factors that contribute to his performance as a salesman?"	"In your opinion, what makes him one of the best salesmen in the industry?"
"Tell me about the range of operating parameters for your equipment?"	"Tell me about the operational limitations of your equipment?"

"Describe for me each precinct in the city?"	"Would you please describe for me the worst precincts in the city?"
"Tell me about what resources you still need that Homeland Security could provide your agency?"	"Tell me about the resources Homeland Security hasn't provided your agency?"

Dealing with Fading Memory

Collecting valid, useful, correct information is the reason you are conducting your debriefing or interview. Otherwise, there is no point. Sometimes, however, fading memories get in the way of collecting that information, especially as more and more time elapses. Asking detailed, probing questions of your interlocutor is one way to prompt your interlocutor to remember the details. What else can you do, though?

Prompt Memories Early On

How many times have you been asked a question, only to remember the correct answer just after the meeting was concluded and the opportunity to respond was lost? This happens more than you might think. With the passage of just a little extra time you recall the answer. How do you, as the collector of information, make sure your contact doesn't experience this? You prompt his memory early on, before you begin with your questions. Just as you would like for your interlocutor to know your objectives, so that he can assist and support you. You can also announce the substantive question areas that interest you. As you proceed, your interlocutor will recall all kinds of thoughts and images. This will assist him in recalling details that he might not surface without prior prompting.

Example of Prompting Memories Early On

Henry	"Peter, I have many questions for you today. Specifically, I'd like to talk about that day three years ago when you and your team responded to the accident in Mather Gorge."
Peter	"I'm not sure how much help I can be. I filed all the reports, but We've done a lot since then. I'll do what I can to remember."
Henry	"I understand. I don't need much more information. I'm specifically tying to get a better feel for the weather at the time you were repelling down to the victim."
Peter	"Yeah, I can do that. What else are you looking for?"

Henry	"Well, before we get to that, I'd like to ask a few questions about your team members, there training, the organization of the team by specialization, and where they are assigned now."
Peter	"Sure."

Schedules and Agendas

If you are dealing with an interlocutor on a regular basis, you will undoubtedly develop stronger and stronger rapport. Use this to your advantage to ask for him to bring his schedule/agenda book to your meetings. If you have questions about dates, he may just be able to oblige by opening up the book to the date in question, thus prompting his memory. You also never know what other valuable information may be contained therein. Company schedule/agenda/date books may contain company data, photographs of facilities, and more.

Relive the Experience

Another way to prompt your interlocutor to remember details is to walk him through an experience. Start at the beginning of the experience and ask a series of simple questions designed to determine the time line for the experience. This will build a momentum and prompt memories to come out that your interlocutor may have never thought about. Once you have framed in the time line of the experience, you can the work to fill in the details. This kind of prompting is also a good way to extract detail on the emotions involved in the experience as well, as your interlocutor is reliving it as it happened. This "stream of consciousness" debriefing is quite different from a debriefing organized into neat little subject boxes according to your objectives. Once you complete the debriefing, you might consider breaking the information out into useful pieces.

Example
Relive the Experience

Peter	"Henry, I had such a full schedule that day, I just can't recall everybody who was at the meeting."
Henry	"That's alright Peter. I understand. Instead, why don't you walk me through your day and we'll see what we can come up with. You arrived at the office at 8:30 and the meeting was at 9 o'clock..."
Peter	"Yes, I remember getting to the office late that morning and rushing to get ready."
Henry	"...Rushing to get ready?"
Peter	"Yeah, as I was printing copies of my notes, Winston called to remind me the meeting had been moved up to nine."

Henry	"Yeah, we were both attending in place of our boss. All the offices in the division were included."
Peter	"All the offices?"
Henry	"Yeah, that's right…finance, support, sales, marketing, and research."
Peter	"So, you got there on time?"
Henry	"Well, actually, no. The printer jammed and I got there five minutes late."
Peter	"Late? The others must have been impatient?"
Henry	"Oh, you bet they were! Anderson from sales was complaining. The guy from finance didn't care. He was probably just happy to be away from his boss."
Peter	"Away from his boss?"
Henry	"Yeah, that's Jim Unser. He's a real taskmaster, or so they say."
Peter	"I see…and the guy from finance? He was…?"

Henry	"Oh yeah! That was Mike Dillard! And the marketing rep wasn't there. She came in late too! Janice Hunter I think it was."
Peter	"That accounts for finance, support, sales, and marketing. What about research?"
Henry	"Well...that had to have been Harlan."
Peter	"Harlan?"
Henry	"Yeah, he's the number two in the division. His boss, Jim Carmichael, was away at a conference. I signed off on his travel voucher."
Peter	"So, there were you, Winston, Anderson, Dillard, Hunter and Harlan? Is that it?"
Henry	"Yeah, I think that was all of us."

Start With What You Can Remember and Work Toward The Details

This is similar to reliving the experience, in that you first frame the big picture and then add the detail. It is different from reliving the experience in that you are not looking to collect information on an experience, but rather on something fixed in time. This may include descriptions of facilities, the personnel dynamics of an organization, people and their personalities, or technical issues. Using this technique, you might start prompting your interlocutor with broad questions that are easy for him to answer about the subject of the debriefing. Once you've collected those answers, your interlocutor will begin remembering more and more. In areas in which his memories are not as clear, you can consider adding leading questions.

Start With What You Can Remember and Work Toward The Details

Investigator	"So John, you've said you believe that Miller was one of the people at the scene of the murder. Why was that?"
Witness	"Well, I'm certain he was, I believe I saw him coming from the utility shed after everybody else had departed the field."
Investigator	"You said that you only saw him from behind?"
Witness	"Yes, but he was wearing his uniform shirt. It was bright red with the number 17 on the back."

Investigator	"You believed it was him, because of the color and number?"
Witness	"Yes."
Investigator	"Did you actually his face?"
Witness	"No, I did not."
Investigator	"How could you be certain?"
Witness	"Well, it looked like him, his height, weight and build, you know."
Investigator	"Okay, and anything else…?"
Witness	"Well, now I remember! I recall him going to his car. It was a black BMW! It was his car."
Investigator	"How can you be certain it was his car?"
Witness	"I remember the car, because we all talk about it. It's got a Stanford University sticker on the back window and those ridiculous racing wheels!"

The 5 W's and How

Who? What? When? Where? Why? And How?

These six one-word questions are the most important questions for anybody trying to collect the critical details of any story. When you have answered these questions, you have all the details you need. Memorize and recite 'The 5 W's and How' and you will be able to prompt yourself in any situation to collect the critical information you need.

The 5 W's and How

Who	is involved?	Personalities
What	did he do?	Actions
Where	did he do it?	Location
When	did he do it?	Time
Why	did he do it?	Motivations
How	did he do it?	Quality

Keep in mind that you may not wish to actually ask 'The 5 W's and How' in quick succession. If you do, you may come across to your subject as an interrogator. Remember, you are trying to build a relationship with your subject. As an alternative to actually asking the questions, try using 'The 5 W's and How' as a guideline that you keep in your mind. As you collect what you need, check off the answers to 'The 5W's and How.' If one particular questions is not being answered, then you may direct a specific question to your subject.

Example of The 5 W's and How

Notice in this example how the investigator obtains answers to his questions without asking them outright. In this way, he can check off the key pieces of the witness' account asking overly intrusive questions unless necessary.

What & How	
Investigator	"Why don't you tell me what happened?"
Where	
Witness	"Well, I was in the office in the back when I heard what I thought was a customer coming into the shop. I expected Marie would take care of the customer. A few moments later though, I heard him yell at her and thought something was wrong. I got up, went up front and it was then that I saw her on the ground. I helped her: she was bleeding from her scalp. She then pointed to the cash register."
Who	
Investigator	"So the assailant hit Marie? Was he a big guy?"

Witness	"Yeah, he was big, about six foot three, broad shoulders, lean though. He was well built."
Investigator	"What did he look like?"
Witness	"He was light-skinned with red hair, a long thin nose, and a moustache. He was very Irish looking. He was wearing a long sleeve jacket, but I saw tattooing up around his neck, from the collar up the back of his neck."
What	
Investigator	"What did Marie indicate by pointing to the cash register?"
Witness	"She wanted me to see that the drawer was out of the register and on the ground, that the attacker had stolen our day's cash."
When	
Investigator	"And this was before closing?"
Witness	"Yes."
When	
Investigator	"And that would have been...?"

Witness	"Oh, about 5:50 p.m."
Why	
Investigator	"Why do you think he chose your shop?"
Witness	"Well, we do have more customer traffic than most of the other stores in the center. That might be it, but most of our sales are by credit card. He didn't get away with much cash."
Investigator	"Did he walk away with any sales slips with credit card numbers on them?"
Witness	"I didn't think to check that!"
Where	
Investigator	"I have one last question. Which way did he escape after the robbery?"
Witness	"Oh, yeah, he went straight out the door to his getaway car. He drove away to the south."

Fact vs. Comment

Fact and Commentary are Not the Same
This is a simple, no nonsense statement. However, it bears mention up front, because people will often and easily confuse the two, regardless of how well educated they are.

- **Fact is that which exists, or happened. It is irrefutable and not subject to interpretation.**

- **Commentary is the supposition, conjecture, analysis or opinion that can be added to a fact.**

Fact	Commentary
"Yesterday the Prime Minister flew from Nova Scotia to Newfoundland."	"I believe the Prime Minister in Newfoundland. This explains his departure from Nova Scotia."
	"The Prime Minister must prefer Newfoundland over Nova Scotia."

Is either of these statements true? They might be. However, if the only facts we have at our disposal are represented in the initial statement, then we have no way of determining whether they are true or not. Much of the validity of the commentary depends upon the expertise of your subject. For example, the first comment might carry greater weight if it came from the Prime Minister's secretary, as opposed to an investment banker in London. The second comment might carry more weight if it came from the Prime Minister's wife, as opposed to Newfoundland's director of tourism.

Here are a few more examples.

Fact vs. Comment

Fact	Comment
"Jim came back from New Orleans yesterday."	"I believe Jim came back from New Orleans yesterday."
"Frank announced that the reports would be available at 10 am."	"Frank commented to me he believed the reports would be available at 10am."
"What time did he leave for the meeting?"	"What time do you think it was when he left for the meeting?"
"What were Robert's reasons for pulling out of the Anderson contract?"	"Tell me what you think of Robert's decision to pull out of the Anderson contract?"

"Who is the primary decision maker we need to meet to push our proposal forward?"	"Who do you think we need to meet to push our proposal forward?"

Even Experts Will Tend to Blend Them

Fact vs. Comment: There is a significant difference between fact and commentary. Your subject, although probably able to distinguish between the two, may have a tendency to provide all information as well sourced and factual. After all, he is the expert you sought out. His opinion, therefore, becomes every bit as "factual" as the facts. Do not take your subject completely at his word. Ask clarifying questions about the sourcing of his information. Determine what is known. Collect facts. Determine what is commentary based on factual events or data. Commentary is often enlightening (sometimes as much as the facts). To the degree it is based on experience and expertise, it is important to collect.

Distinguish Fact from Commentary with Clarifying Questions

Distinguishing fact from commentary is not difficult, as long as you make a conscious effort to do so. This can be as simple as asking clarifying questions of your interlocutor. You might perceive such questions to be rude or intrusive. However, your interlocutor will usually appreciate the fact that you are attempting to understand the substance of your debriefing or interview in greater nuance, and will assist you in attaining that understanding. Clarifying questions to distinguish between fact and commentary might sound like this.

"I'm very interested in how you view this matter, would you make the distinction between your view and those of others?"
"The facts seem to indicate something quite different. What is your opinion based on those facts?"
"Could you provide me a chronological listing of the events and then tell me how you think they're important?"

The most important issue to consider in differentiating between fact and commentary is the sourcing of the information. In other words, is your subject providing you facts that he knows to be facts? Do others know those facts in addition to your subject? Were they derived from his work or research? Is he providing his own supposition and/or analysis based on those facts?

Clarifying Questions

Jim	"So, as I stated previously, Johnson was the first to develop the idea and the technique of employing masking agents to cover up the scent of the narcotics to fool the dogs. He did it at his lab in the mountains west of Chihuahua. He was working for the Juarez Cartel."
Paul	"That's interesting Jim. I knew he was working near Chihuahua, but I'm still a bit confused. I thought Gutierrez was the cartel guy who developed that idea?"
Jim	"That's what most believe, because Gutierrez is the chemist now. He's the guy who was Johnson's assistant at that time. He's also the guy who killed Johnson later on. He circulated the idea that he was the one."
Paul	"Are there any other interpretations?"
Jim	"There may be many, but I know that for certain. Gutierrez and I were drinking together at the time. In a drunken stupor one night he boasted that he'd stolen the credit after he made it look like the Sinaloans had killed Johnson."

Paul	"I don't understand why he would do that?"
Jim	"Well, his cousin was in tight with one of the cartel bosses. Together, they wanted to move up in the cartel. Killing Johnson and taking credit for his work was one way to do that."
Paul	"And Gutierrez said that too?"
Jim	"No, he didn't. I suspect that to be the case based on what he told me, that his cousin was supportive of him and wanted better for their whole family."

Don't Forget to Seek Commentary

We've just talked about the critical need to differentiate between fact and commentary. It is CRITICAL. This, however, does not mean that commentary is less useful than fact. In reality, commentary can be enormously useful. If you are missing pieces of the information puzzle, commentary, opinion, and analysis can provide much greater understanding of the substantive issues. If an expert in the subject matter is providing commentary based on long years of experience, the commentary can assist in understanding the nature of the issue. In fact, it can be even more useful in trying to draw conclusions as to what will happen in the future. Don't forget to seek commentary when and where it is warranted.

Hypothetical Questions

149

The final point we wish to make about fact and commentary concerns what we'll call hypothetical questions. The name tells you exactly what they are: questions designed to elicit hypothetical responses to hypothetical situations. These are the ultimate elicitors of commentary, as opposed to fact, as they seek considered commentary from your interlocutor on a possible situation. Just as with other commentary seeking questions, the validity and authoritativeness of the response depends to a great degree on the expertise of your interlocutor. But, there is one thing that sets hypothetical questions apart from other kinds of questions.

If you are concerned with collecting intelligence information, whether to support sales and marketing efforts or to monitor your competition, or both, hypothetical questions can be employed with great effectiveness to provide about future courses of action. Let's look at what some hypothetical questions might look like. We think you'll see how they can become a powerful technique in your panoply of interviewing and debriefing tools.

Examples of Hypothetical Questions

"If you had to make a decision on that issue, knowing what you know, what would you do?"

"If you were to experience a sharp downturn in revenues, how would your firm fund its basic research?"

"If you were in her position, what would you do?"

"How would you view a sharp increase in share of market in your top two competitors? How would you respond."

Divergent vs. Leading Questions

Divergent: Elicit Detailed, Thoughtful Responses

Divergent questioning is the skill of asking open-ended questions, which prompt the development of creativity in problem solving. Divergent questions are those, which do not seek a "yes/no" response, but rather encourage your subject to respond with a thorough, detailed answer. This type of question encourages multiple responses, and a detailed exploration of concepts and ideas. It is a way for you to encourage an open-minded examination of an issue. It also leads to fuller responses. Divergent questioning requires you to put more thought and preparation into the questions you ask.

Examples of Divergent vs. Leading Questions

Divergent	Leading
"Would you please describe for me what happened during the argument?"	"Did you witness the argument?"
"Just how crowded was the corridor? "	"Were there a lot of people in the corridor?"
"Why did you arrive late?"	"Did you arrive late?"

"Please describe for me the man who fired the gun?"	"Is he the man who fired the gun?"
"What color was the car?"	"Was the car red?"
" Who were the conference attendees?"	"Were they at the conference?"

Examples of Divergent Questions

Tim	"Last week, you attended the conference, what were your overall impressions of it?"
Brian	"Well, I found it interesting, because we were able to talk with our counterparts in other states, compare our operations with theirs and come up with some new ideas."

Tim	"I would be very interested in your analysis of the market?"
Brian	"Sure, but I'm really not qualified. You might ask…"

Tim	"What were the announcements that the CEO made yesterday?"

Brian	"Well, he began by announcing the latest personnel changes, then moved on to our financial performance, ..."
Tim	"What were your sales figures for this quarter?"
Brian	"Our figures were low due to the sluggishness in housing start ups."

Leading: Elicit Yes/No Responses

Leading, or Closed, Questions are those questions, which prompt your subject to provide you with a "yes/no" response, or simplistic responses of only a few words in specific response to your question. We recommend that you avoid asking these types of questions in most circumstances, as they really provide little in the way of useful information. Essentially, you are seeking a confirmation or denial of something you already know or think you know. Leading questions do not really enhance your knowledge and do not promote critical thinking. They are the opposite of divergent questions.

Examples of Leading Questions

Paula	"Did you attend the trade show last week?"
Tammy	"Yes."

Paula	"Can you tell me about the performance of the market?
Tammy	"No."

Paula	"Did the CEO make any announcements yesterday?"
Tammy	"Yes."

Paula	"Did you have good sales figures this quarter?"
Tammy	"No."

Laddering

Laddering is a simple technique that we have adopted from the repertory grid elicitation techniques of psychologist George Kelly and his personal construct theory. Kelly developed the laddering technique to delve deeper into the details of a patient's life without injecting bias into his follow up questions. A characteristic of laddering is that the follow up questions you ask become more and more focused, while the responses become stronger and more intense. You may use your laddering technique in two directions: upward laddering using 'why' questions, and downward laddering using 'how' questions.

Upward Laddering with 'Why'

Upward laddering employs 'why' questions to elicit preferences and then the reasons behind those preferences. This allows you to move upward through a series of comparisons so as to arrive at broader and broader conclusions.

Keep in mind that while this technique can provide much detailed information, it also has a tendency to produce a fair degree of COMMENTARY, as well as fact. These are things you need to differentiate, as you collect.

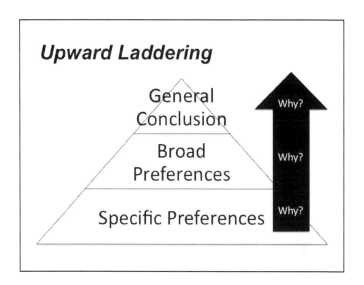

Example of Upward Laddering

In this example, you can see that Frank, using simple "why" questions, is able to prompt Dave to provide a great deal of detailed information from the interview. His questions are almost complete restatements of Dave's responses, which prompting Dave to carefully consider the subject of discussion and provide well thought out responses. Frank's use of Dave's own words in his questions also reduces the possibility that he will inject bias into his questions.

Dave	"Alpha Inc. is without a doubt the leading firm in the dictionary publishing industry. The Beta and Delta Companies are just not capable of competing with it."
Frank	"That's interesting. Why would you assess that Alpha is the leading firm?"
Dave	"Alpha is the leading firm, because it constantly comes up with the most innovative business ideas."
Frank	"Why do they constantly come up with the most innovative business ideas?"
Dave	"I believe Alpha's marketing department understands the changing nature of the publishing business."
Frank	"Why do you believe Alpha's marketing department understands the changing nature of the publishing business?"
Dave	"I think they understand that computer-based, online and smart phone-based reference products are the wave of the future."
Frank	"This is all quite interesting. Why do you think they understand the market so well?"

Dave	"Well, I think they've employed young marketers who understand the changing use of technology. Their senior executives understand this and have let their young Turks lead the form into the future."

Downward Laddering with 'How'

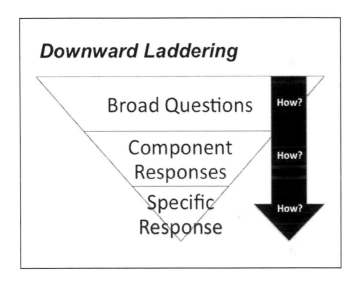

Downward laddering employs 'how' questions, allowing you to take a very broad subject and break it down into component parts for more detailed examination. These questions usually take the form "Tell me more about how (one component differs from the other)."

Example of Downward Laddering

In this example, Thomas asks Jenny to provide the names of the two most important people in her industry. Once Thomas elicited the basic outlines of Jenny's response, he used a series of 'how' questions to branch into two lines of questioning: one to explore John's personality, and the other to explore Wendy's. If he so desired, he could have asked questions that broke the topics down into smaller and smaller compartments until he understood in ever increasing detail the many facets of John and Wendy's personalities.

Thomas	"Jenny, please tell me who the two most important personalities in your industry happen to be, and why they are so important."
Jenny	"I would say they are John Jeffers and Wendy Hart. John is important, because he has the vision to see where the industry is going. Wendy is important, because she has the ability to take an under performing company and turn it around into a profitable business."
Thomas	"John and Wendy clearly have different skill sets. Tell me more about how they are different."

Jenny	"Well, John has a very creative personality, while Wendy has an organized way of doing things."
Thomas	"In terms of his creativity, how does John differ from Wendy?"
Jenny	"I would say John has a penchant for thinking out of the box and seeking unconventional solutions to conventional problems. On the other hand, Wendy seems to know how to take the knowledge of others and apply it to solve problems."

Loaded Questions

Loaded questions are those questions, which either channel your contact to answer your questions within a range of possibilities, or prompt him to provide a response with negative or positive slants. Typically in a debriefing or interview, an interviewer may unknowingly employ loaded questions and increase the possibility of leading the contact to provide incorrect or inaccurate information. While loaded questions have their uses, we would recommend that you avoid asking loaded questions for general interviewing and debriefing scenarios.

There are instances, however, in which loaded questions can be used intentionally to prompt a contact for accurate, objective information. They can even be used to test your contact, to determine whether or not he is providing you with false information, whether wittingly or unwittingly. Those instances deal with individuals who tend to withhold, or are suspected of providing false, information – not the types of situations we generally envision within a business context. As for testing your contact suspected of providing false information, the key is to choose specific questions for which you already know the responses. Once you have done this, there are two general ways to proceed.

First, you may choose to test your contact's veracity without confronting him. In other words, you ask him the question and collect the response he provides. Knowing the response to be false, you say nothing and move on. This allows you the freedom to analyze the effect of the false information before proceeding. Once you have done so, you can determine whether to use the situation for competitive disinformation purposes, or to avoid further contact.

Second, you may choose to confront your contact with the knowledge that he has provided false information. This is obviously a drastic measure in that it will likely end the interview and the relationship right there – the information flow thus ends. This all but assures that you telegraph to your contact that you know he is providing false or misleading information. While this might nullify the damage of any possible disinformation effort, it leaves you no way to take advantage of the opportunity.

Examples of Loaded Questions
Both of these questions are loaded in the sense that they lead your interlocutor to a particular response. In the first example, the question makes a link between hard work and the resulting rewards and satisfaction. This creates a bias in the response toward explaining why or how hard work results in rewards and satisfaction. The question does not allow for the interlocutor to consider that hard work may not result in rewards and satisfaction. In the second example, the question leads the interlocutor to the conclusion that Omega management's decisions were incorrect and lead to slow growth. The response was predictable, i.e. the interlocutor tried to explain the company's slow

growth in stock value by the less than optimal performance of management. However, isn't it possible that the slow growth in the company's stock value was the desired result of management's decisions?

Loaded Questions	
John	"Can you tell me how working hard can lead to a life of satisfaction and rewards?"
George	"Working hard leads to accomplishing the goals you set for yourself. Achieving your goals is satisfying and leads to rewards."
Kevin	"Over the last year, Omega Computer's stock value has experienced slow growth. Could you please provide me your thoughts on how the decisions of Omega's senior management have resulted in this slow growth?"
Will	"Well, I would estimate that its decisions did not make sense within the context of its competitors' moves in the marketplace."

Rather than ask the questions as above, you might consider wording your questions as follows:

John	"Can you tell me what attributes lead to a life of satisfaction and rewards?"
George	"Of course most will say a life of hard work leads to a life of satisfaction and reward, but I think it also comes from having a talent for the work you do and then enjoying your work."
Kevin	"Over the last year, Omega Computer's stock value has experienced slow growth. Could you please provide me your thoughts on why that is the case?"
Will	"Well, I believe Omega has lost its ability to develop new products that respond to consumer wants and needs. They're relying on a marketing department that is rooted in the desktop world and isn't moving in the direction of mobile computing."

Broad vs. Narrow Focus

Broadly focused questions are used to prompt your subject for general information about a particular topic. They allow you to determine the areas in which your subject has valid, accurate information. Conversely, narrowly focused questions are used to dig for specific pieces of information within the framework of the broader questions.

We liken the use of broadly and narrowly focused questions to the use of the continually narrowing filters used by archeologists at a dig. First, archeologists will use excavators to remove large amounts of earth in which there is little chance of finding much of value. Next, they use shovels to remove layers of earth closer to their target areas. Finally, they will resort to the use of hand tools, toothbrushes, etc. to avoid breaking artifacts. This is an excellent analogy for the use of broadly focused questions to identify the scope of information your subject has. As the focus of your questions narrows, you then begin to seek smaller, yet more valuable, pieces of information.

Alternatively, you can also broad and narrow questions depending upon your subject and the way he looks at the world. Some people look strategically at the world and consider their place within it based on broad issues. For these people, broadly focused questions are much more practical.

Others are more finely attuned to what they do within their own spheres of influence. They do not often consider the 'bigger picture' seeing what they do as the core of their existence. For these people, narrowly focused questions will tend to elicit better, more detailed responses.

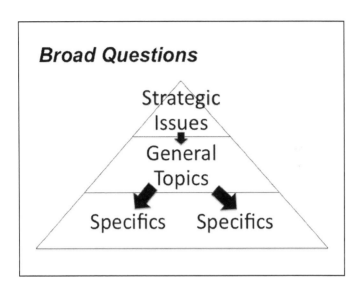

Example of Broad Focus

William	"Devon, could you please tell me about the topics you believe are the most important for me to understand as I learn about psychology?"

Devon	"Well, first off you've got to understand that psychology is a social science discipline that attempts to understand human behavior and mental function. It is a far reaching field."
William	"How far reaching?"
Devon	"Well, we study topics including human perception, motivations and emotions, cognition, attention, and interpersonal relationships."
William	"That is far reaching! I get the sense that research developments could have an impact in almost every field. Where do you see yourself fitting into the bigger picture?"
Devon	"That's a good question. I'm what we call a cognitive psychologist. I study human problem solving, learning, perception...the way people's minds process information."
William	"That sounds ominous! What does that mean in practical terms?"

Devon	"Well, what it really means is that we study memory, problem solving and visual processing of information. Personally, I study memory – how people remember, or forget, what they learn."
William	"How do you do that?"
Devon	"I conduct research experiments that seek to learn how much information people can absorb at a time, how fast they do it, how much detail they can retain, how much is too much, that kind of thing."

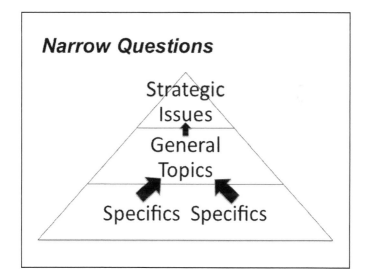

Example of Narrow Focus

William	"So Devon, I understand you're a researcher? What kind do you do?"
Devon	"I do psychology experiments to determine the extent of human memory."
William	"Why do you do those kinds of experiments?"
Devon	"We're trying to determine the extent of memory, the manners in which we solve problems and how we process visual inputs."
William	"So that makes you a cognitive psychologist, right?"
Devon	"Exactly."
William	"I thought so. But there's something I don't understand. How does cognitive psychology fit into the various areas of psychological research?"
Devon	"Good question. Psychology on the whole seeks to study human behavior and mental functions. I'd like to think cognitive psychology is the central research area, the core on which all other areas depend."

About the Author

Frank Stopa is a former Central Intelligence Agency operations officer who worked and negotiated successfully with law enforcement, military and intelligence services worldwide during his career. He has also served as an adjunct terrorism instructor for the California Emergency Management Agency's California Specialized Training Institute, the California Commission on Police Officer Standards and Training (POST), and the Northern California Regional Public Safety Training College in Sacramento, California. Frank currently writes and works as a counter terrorism instructor for law enforcement officers, fire fighters, and fusion center officials across the United States under the auspices of Knowledge and Intelligence Program Professionals of Long Beach, California.

Made in the USA
Charleston, SC
10 December 2010